※※※※

THE CASE

OF THE

PIGLET'S

PATERNITY

※※※※

A Driftless Connecticut Series Book

This book is a 2015 selection in the
Driftless Connecticut Series, for an outstanding
book in any field on a Connecticut topic
or written by a Connecticut author.

Jon C. Blue

THE CASE

OF THE

PIGLET'S

PATERNITY

Trials from the
New Haven Colony,
1639–1663

Wesleyan University Press
Middletown, Connecticut

Wesleyan University Press
Middletown CT 06459
www.wesleyan.edu/wespress
© 2015 Jon C. Blue
All rights reserved
Manufactured in the United States of America
Designed by Mindy Basinger Hill
Typeset in Adobe Jenson Pro

The Driftless Connecticut Series is funded by the
Beatrice Fox Auerbach Foundation Fund
at the Hartford Foundation for Public Giving.

Wesleyan University Press is a member of the
Green Press Initiative. The paper used in this book meets
their minimum requirement for recycled paper.

Library of Congress Cataloging-in-Publication Data

Blue, Jon C., author.
The case of the piglet's paternity : trials from the
New Haven colony, 1639–1663 / Jon C. Blue.
pages   cm
Includes bibliographical references and index.
ISBN 978-0-8195-7537-1 (cloth : alk. paper) —
ISBN 978-0-8195-7538-8 (ebook)
1. Trials—New-Haven Colony—History.
2. Trials—Connecticut—History.
3. Justice, Administration of—Connecticut—History.
4. Law—New-Haven Colony—History.
I. Title.
KF220.B58 2015
347.746'0709032—dc23   2014048332

5   4   3   2   1

FOR JEAN

CONTENTS

THE CASE

OF THE

PIGLET'S

PATERNITY

Introduction

꧁꧂

THE

NEW HAVEN

TRIALS

꧁꧂

The opening scenes tell us we are in another world. A human head is pitched on a pole in the marketplace. A man is hanged because he is deemed to be the father of a piglet. Other events could happen in any era. A gun explodes, injuring an eye. A woman's reputation is slandered. All of these events, great and small, occurred at the dawn of American history, in a short-lived colony little remembered today.

We know of these events because they happened as a result of trials held in the New Haven Colony in the middle of the seventeenth century. The trials were remarkable not only because of their subject matter but also because of the way they were conducted and recorded. Following centuries of obscurity, the trials contained in the colony's records are brought to light in this book.

The most engaging aspect of the New Haven trials is the vivid manner of their reporting. The long-ago secretaries responsible for recording the transactions of the colony were not content to use the dry, succinct language of official documents so common at that or any other time—"John Jones was convicted of murder and sentenced to death."[1] Instead, the New Haven secretaries had the skill and genius to put flesh on these bones and fill them with life. We don't just hear the names of judges and litigants. We sit in the front row and hear the twists and turns of fortune as the participants battle with life and liberty at stake. We see witnesses squirm on the stand when confronted with evidence contradicting their testimony.[2] We hear the court denounce a defendant (unhappily, a twelve-year-old boy) as "a notorious lying boy, a great offense to the English amongst whom he lives, and a dishonor to the nation to which he belongs" (see chapter 28, "The Milford Arson Case"). We watch the court at its Solomonic best, reasoning with a widow who is about to receive her deceased husband's entire estate at the expense of his minor children: the court asks her how she would feel if her husband had given everything to her children and nothing to her (see chapter 18, "The Disputed Will"). We observe the court at its bone-chilling worst, ordering a small girl to be publicly whipped and sold into servitude (see chapter 33, "The Burning Barn"). In all these instances, we are spectators watching real dramas involving recognizable human beings, in all their wisdom and in all their folly. The records of the New Haven Colony captured these moments in a way that few judicial documents have ever done.

And then darkness. The records were not written for publication, and their authors could not have anticipated that anyone, at least anyone in future generations, would ever read them. They were written in a close and sometimes difficult seventeenth-century hand on folio sheets and then stored away in the anonymity of a local clerk's repositories. There, they were almost forgotten, and several years of their contents were eventually lost.[3]

In 1772, the Connecticut General Assembly passed a surprising archival enactment:

> Whereas the first antient [ancient] book of records of this Colony remaining in the Secretary's office and the first records of the Jurisdiction of New Haven in the office of the town-clerk of the town of New Haven are much worn and decayed, and by constant use in danger of being totally ruined: Resolved by this Assembly, that the Secretary be directed, and he is hereby directed, to procure the said records to be fairly transcribed into some proper book or books to be by him procured for that purpose and laid before this Assembly to be compared and duly authenticated for common use: to the end that the said original ancient records may be safely preserved and used only upon special and important occasions. The Secretary is also directed to receive into his hands and deposit in his office the antient book of records of the Jurisdiction of New Haven now remaining in the office of the clerk of the county court of New Haven county, who is also hereby requested to deliver the same to him accordingly, that the same may remain for publick use in the publick archives of the Colony.[4]

Although the records of the Colony of Connecticut were duly preserved and transcribed pursuant to this act, the New Haven records were not. They remained in the custody of local officials, eventually being placed in a copper box.[5]

There matters stood until 1856. In that year, the Connecticut General Assembly passed the following act:

> *Resolved*, That the secretary be authorized to purchase for the use of the state, two hundred and fifty copies of the proposed publication of the records of the Colony of New Haven, prior to

the union with Connecticut, transcribed and edited by Charles J. Hoadly, Esq. *Provided,* that such publication shall be authenticated by the official certificate of the secretary, as a true copy of the original record; *and provided also,* that the expense of the same shall not exceed two dollars and fifty cents per volume.

Resolved, That the copies so purchased be distributed as follows: one copy to the town clerk of each town in this state, to be preserved in his office for the use of the town; one copy to the governor, and to each of the state officers of this state; one copy to the governor of each of the several states and territories of the United States, to be deposited in their several state libraries; one copy to the library of congress; one copy to the Smithsonian Institute; twenty five copies to Mr. Alexander Vattemare for international exchange; and the remainder of the said two hundred and fifty copies to be deposited in the office of the secretary, subject to the disposal of the general assembly.[6]

Charles J. Hoadly, the Connecticut state librarian, took his job seriously. He painstakingly transcribed and printed the New Haven records, retaining the contractions and abbreviations found in the original manuscript, and published them in two volumes. The first volume, covering the years 1638 to 1649, was published in 1857. The second volume, covering 1653 to 1664, was published in 1858.[7] (The manuscript for the years 1649 to 1653 was lost.)

Prodigious though the effort behind these volumes was, three criticisms of the printed version are in order. First, the retention of the contractions and abbreviations of the original manuscript, however valuable to scholars, makes the end result extremely difficult to read. A modern reader must spend a great deal of time attempting to decipher what is actually being said in the proceedings described. Second, four cases involving sexual matters were redacted from the published work "as containing matters of a nature unfit for publication."[8] Third, the limitation of publication to 250 volumes, most of them consigned to scattered government repositories, virtually guaranteed that the records would continue to languish in practical obscurity.[9] It is hoped that the present work will resolve these issues.

The original manuscript of the New Haven records, consisting of approximately 250 folio-size pages, remains in the archives of the Connecticut State Library.

History of the Colony

A comprehensive history of the New Haven Colony is beyond the scope of this work,[10] but some knowledge of that history is essential to understanding the trials conducted under the colony's authority.

The Colony of New Haven, which existed from its founding in 1638 to its union with the neighboring Connecticut Colony in 1665, resulted from a lifelong friendship between two English Puritans. John Davenport, a vicar of the English church, and Theophilus Eaton, a wealthy London merchant, were, in Cotton Mather's indelible phrase, the "Moses and Aaron" of the new community.[11]

Davenport (1597–1670) was a nonconformist, seeking to conform the church to biblical rules. Puritans like himself fell into disfavor under Charles I, and many of them looked to New England with the idea of founding biblically based communities there. Davenport's childhood friend Eaton (1590–1658) had become wealthy through trade in Europe and was attracted by the possibilities of additional trade in the new world. "Thus a secular as well as a religious interest prompted the enterprise."[12]

Under the leadership of Davenport and Eaton, a company of believers and traders sailed for Boston in 1637. Their stay in the Massachusetts Bay Colony appears not to have been congenial, and in 1638 they departed that colony to establish their own settlement at Quinnipiack Harbor on the northern shore of Long Island Sound, the location of modern-day New Haven.

For about a year, the colonists were occupied in building their new town, planting fields, and establishing an uneasy truce with the native inhabitants. In 1639, they turned to the task of establishing the rules by which the "plantation" was to be governed.

On June 4, 1639, the freemen of the plantation, about seventy in number, met in a large barn in New Haven "to consult about settling civil Government according to God."[13] It was agreed that "the Scriptures do hold forth a perfect rule for the direction and government of all men in all duties which they are to perform to God and men."[14] A "fundamental agreement" was made that "Church members only shall be free burgesses, and they only shall choose among themselves magistrates and officers to have the power of transacting all public civil affairs of this plantation, of making and repealing laws, dividing inheritances, deciding of differences that may arise, and doing all things and business of like nature."[15]

On October 25, 1639, seven men "who were in the foundation of the church" met to establish a formal civil government.[16] These pillars of the church proceeded to recognize a "court"[17] consisting of "all those that have been received into the fellowship of this church since the gathering of it" plus members of other "approved" churches.[18] The "fundamental agreement" of 1639 was recognized as the basis of the plantation's government.

Theophilus Eaton was chosen as "magistrate" for the term of one year. His charge, given to him by Davenport, was that of Deuteronomy 1:16–17: "Hear the causes between your brethren, and judge righteously between every man and his brother, and the stranger that is with him. Ye shall not respect persons in judgment; but ye shall hear the small as well as the great; ye shall not be afraid of the face of man; for the judgment is God's: and the cause that is too hard for you, bring it unto me, and I will hear it."

Robert Newman, Matthew Gilbert, Nathaniel Turner, and Thomas Fugill were chosen as "deputies" to assist the magistrate. Thomas Fugill was also chosen as "public notary." His obligation in that capacity was "to attend court and from time to time to keep a faithful record of all passages and conclusions of the court." Fugill's faithful adherence to this task established a tradition of excellence in reporting that has made the present work possible. Robert Seely was chosen as "marshal." His charge was "from time to time to warn courts according to the direction of the magistrate, to serve and execute warrants, to attend the court at all times, and to be ready and diligent in his person or by his deputy to execute the sentences of the court." All officers were to be elected annually at a "General Court" of the plantation to be held during the last week of October.[19]

Prior to 1643, the term "New Haven" pertained to the town of that name. After that year, the name referred both to the town and to the more expansive "New Haven Colony."[20] The colony now encompassed a total of six towns: the town of New Haven, the towns of Branford and Guilford to the east, the towns of Milford and Stamford to the west, and the town of Southold on the North Fork of Long Island.[21]

On October 27, 1643, the magistrates and deputies of the six towns entered into a "fundamental order" elaborating on the "fundamental agreement" of 1639. Only "planters" who were members of "approved churches" were to be "free burgesses" with the right to vote. Only church members could occupy positions of "power or trust," although all free planters would have the right "to their inheritance and to commerce."[22]

The free burgesses of each town were to choose church members to be "ordinary judges, to hear and determine all inferior causes." This latter term referred to civil cases involving less than twenty pounds and criminal cases involving corporal punishment or minor fines. Appeals from these judges could be made to the Court of Magistrates for the entire jurisdiction.

The Court of Magistrates consisted of the governor of the colony, the deputy governor, and magistrates elected by the free burgesses of the towns. The court was to meet twice a year in New Haven "for the trial of weighty and capital cases" and the hearing of appeals from the ordinary judges of the towns. Its decisions were subject to appeal to the General Court.

The General Court was "the last and highest" for the jurisdiction. It consisted of the governor, the deputy governor, all of the magistrates in the jurisdiction, and two deputies for each town, chosen by the free burgesses of that town. The General Court convened twice a year, on the first Wednesday in April and the last Wednesday in October. Its charge was to "with all care and diligence provide for the maintenance of the purity of religion and suppress the contrary." It also had the power to make and repeal laws and to execute such laws throughout the colony.[23]

The General Court was thus not simply a judicial court of highest jurisdiction. The modern notion, drawn from Montesquieu, of separate legislative, executive, and judicial authorities,[24] had no application to the New Haven Colony. The General Court combined all three functions in the same governing body.

Theophilus Eaton was elected governor of the colony. He would hold that position until his death in 1658.

In 1645, the General Court pronounced that "it was agreed, concluded and settled as fundamental law, not to be disputed or questioned hereafter, that the judicial laws of God, as they were delivered by Moses, and expounded in other parts of scripture, so far as they are a fence to the moral law . . . shall be accounted of moral and binding equity and force, and as God shall help shall be a constant direction for all proceedings here and a general rule in all courts of Justice how to judge betwixt party and party and how to punish offenders, till the same may be branched out into particulars hereafter."[25] We shall see to what extent this official principle actually guided the colony's jurisprudence.

Prior to 1656, the General Court's 1645 statement of "fundamental law" provided the official standard by which the magistrates of the New Haven Colony were to be guided in their decisions. No printed compilation of statutes existed. While the biblical standard proved helpful (perhaps too helpful) in some cases—notably bestiality cases, which were governed by specific scriptural edict—it was of minimal practical assistance in the much wider array of cases to which no specific biblical rule applied. The absence of jurisprudential standards gave the magistrates great discretion in deciding cases of the latter description.

At some point in the mid-1650s, the General Court asked the governor to provide for a more detailed set of laws. The records of the General Court for May 30, 1655, state that the governor being formerly desired by this Court to view over the laws of this jurisdiction and draw up those of them which he thinks will be most necessary to continue as laws here and compile them together fit to be printed, which being done, were now read, considered, and by vote confirmed, and ordered to be printed. . . . The Court further desired the governor to send for one of the new book of laws in the Massachusetts Colony, and to view over a small book of laws newly come from England, which is said to be Mr. Cotton's, and to add what is already done as he shall think fit, and then the Court will meet again to confirm them, but in the meantime (when they are finished) they desire the elders of the jurisdiction may have the sight of them for their approbation also.[26]

The "new book of laws" referred to was the 1648 Code of the Massachusetts Colony.[27] That work was enormously influential, inspiring both the Code of Laws published by the Connecticut Colony in 1650[28] and the 1656 New Haven Laws.

By October 19, 1655, the governor had completed his task. The records of the General Court for that day state that "the laws which at the Court's desire have been drawn up by the Governor, viewed and considered by the elders of the Jurisdiction, were now read and seriously weighed by this Court, and by vote concluded and ordered to be sent to England to be printed, with such oaths, forms, and precedents as the Governor shall think meet to put in."[29]

The laws of the New Haven Colony were printed in London in 1656.[30] Their introductory statement of law, echoing that of the 1648 Massachusetts Code, sets forth their governing principle.

No man's life shall be taken away, no man's honor or good name shall be stained, no man shall be deprived of his wife or children, no man's goods or estate shall be taken from him under Color or Countenance of Authority, unless it be by virtue or equity of some express Law of this Jurisdiction established by the General Court and sufficiently published, or for want of a Law in any particular case, by word of God, either in the Court of Magistrates or some Plantation Court, according to the weight and value of the cause, only all Capital causes, concerning life or banishment where there is no express Law, shall be judged according to the word and Law of God by the General Court.[31]

The 1656 Laws are thus not intended to provide an exclusive codification of legal rules. While printed laws are to govern when applicable, where there is a "want of a Law" the "word of God" will fill in the gaps.

On June 25, 1656, the governor informed the Court of Magistrates that five hundred "law books" had arrived by ship. The books were ordered to be divided among the constituent towns of the colony, for which each town was obliged to pay twelve pence a copy.[32]

The 1656 Laws proved to be of little practical consequence. While they may have been consulted behind the scenes, they were rarely cited as authority in the colony's judicial rulings (see chapter 18, "The Disputed Will" and chapter 20, "The Stolen Silverware"). As far as the New Haven courts were concerned, both before and after 1656, the governing authority was that of the Bible.

THE UNION WITH THE CONNECTICUT COLONY

In 1662, Charles II issued a charter to the Connecticut Colony. Under the charter, the Connecticut Colony, which previously bordered the New Haven Colony to the north, was now bounded "on the South by the Sea."[33]

The 1662 Charter proved to be a deathblow to the New Haven Colony, which no longer enjoyed official existence in the eyes of English officials. A month later, the inhabitants of Southold voted to join the Connecticut Colony. Stamford and Guilford soon followed. Milford left in 1664, leaving Branford and New Haven to hold out to the bitter end.[34]

The last recorded New Haven trial was conducted in 1663, as recounted in chapter 33, "The Burning Barn." On December 14, 1664, the New Haven Colony gave up the ghost and sent a letter to the Connecticut Colony seeking "love and union between us."[35] On January 5, 1665, the colonies formally united.[36] The New Haven Colony, its government, its laws, and its trials, were now consigned to the dust of history.

The Courts

The New Haven Colony had a three-tiered court system. The Plantation Courts, one for each of the colony's six towns, formed the bottom tier. The Court of Magistrates occupied the middle rung. At the top of the judicial ladder was the General Court.

The records tell us little about the Plantation Courts. It is clear, however, that each town had one or more magistrates elected by the free burgesses of the town. In addition to their task of trying minor civil and criminal cases, the magistrates "examined" parties and witnesses involved in more serious cases and sent records of those examinations to the higher courts.

In contrast, the records tell us a great deal about the General

Court and the Court of Magistrates. They don't tell us everything we'd like to know, but many details can be reconstructed.

THE GENERAL COURT

The General Court, the highest judicial authority in the colony, was not a "court" in the modern sense of the word. As mentioned, under the 1643 fundamental order, the General Court consisted of the governor, the deputy governor, all of the colony's magistrates, and two deputies from each of the colony's six towns.[37] The number of magistrates wasn't fixed,[38] so the membership of the court could vary in size. If each town had one magistrate, the court would have twenty members. But some towns had at least two magistrates, so the total number of officials entitled to sit on the court probably numbered about two dozen.

In practice, not all members actually participated in the General Court's functions. Although the records often fail to describe the court's composition in individual cases, particularly in the colony's early years, the roster of the court is sometimes provided. In the 1656 Case of the Farmhand Arsonist (chapter 19), for example, the court consisted of seventeen members: the governor, the deputy governor, three magistrates (one each from New Haven, Milford, and Guilford), and two deputies each from New Haven, Milford, Guilford, Stamford, Southold, and Branford.[39]

Just as the General Court was not composed of specialized judges, its business was not strictly judicial. There was no strict separation of powers in the New Haven Colony. While the governor had an executive role, he also presided over the upper courts. The General Court combined judicial, legislative, and executive functions. Under the 1643 fundamental order, it had the "power to make and repeal laws and, while they are in force, to require execution of them in the several plantations."[40] It could also "hear and determine all causes."[41] It additionally had the duty to "provide for the maintenance of the purity of religion, and suppress the contrary, according to their best light from the word of God and all wholesome and sound advice which shall be given by the elders and churches in the jurisdiction."[42] The court's business was thus characterized by a wide-ranging array of secular functions along with the combined affairs of church and state.

The records are silent concerning the court's physical circumstances. There was almost certainly no "courthouse" in the modern sense of the word. By tradition, the court first met in a large barn in New Haven.[43] Thereafter, it probably met in a convenient building, such as a church, a house, or a barn. It may have occasionally met outdoors. A record of the February 15, 1660, session of the (much smaller) Court of Magistrates notes that "the season being cold, the Court removed to a private house to consider [the] matter."[44]

Although the General Court differed from the Court of Magistrates in its responsibility for nonjudicial business, there does not appear to have been a strict practical demarcation in the types of judicial business coming before the respective tribunals. Whatever line there was appears to have been chronological. Broadly stated, the General Court had a significantly reduced judicial docket in the colony's later years. Each of the twelve trials reported here occurring between 1639 and 1649 was conducted in the General Court. In contrast, only one of the twenty-one reported trials occurring between 1653 and 1663 was conducted in the General Court: "The Farmhand Arsonist," discussed in chapter 19. The twenty-nine remaining trials from that latter period were conducted in the Court of Magistrates.

THE COURT OF MAGISTRATES

Standing below the General Court in the colony's judicial hierarchy, the Court of Magistrates consisted of "[all] the magistrates for the whole jurisdiction."[45] In addition, the governor and the deputy governor sat on the court ex officio. Because the number of magistrates wasn't fixed, the court didn't have a fixed number of members. There were six towns in the colony, so if each town had one magistrate, the court would have eight members (six magistrates plus the governor and the deputy governor). But some towns had more than one magistrate, so perhaps as many as ten or twelve officials were entitled to sit on the court.

However, as we saw with the General Court, the number of officials actually sitting on the Court of Magistrates was significantly smaller than the number of officials eligible to sit. The court presiding over the 1653 Case of the Rhode Island Privateer (chapter 13), for example, consisted of four members: the governor, the deputy governor, and two magistrates.[46] Sometimes three or four magistrates participated, so a typical Court of Magistrates might contain four to six members.

PROCEDURE

The discussion so far has concerned the formal structure of the New Haven courts. But the modern reader will want to know something quite different. What did the courts look like in operation? If you were transported to a New Haven court by a time machine, what would you see? Who would be in court? Who would speak and when? How did the court reach its decisions? Although the records don't tell us everything—we don't know where people sat or what they wore—they nevertheless tell us a surprising amount. Through them, we see a distinctive type of judicial proceeding, one finding no counterpart either in the modern English-speaking world or, for that matter, elsewhere in the world of the seventeenth century.

The first thing you might notice is that the New Haven courts sat without juries. The rejection of the ancient institution of the jury, well established in England as well as in the Massachusetts and Connecticut colonies, was apparently made at the suggestion of Governor Eaton.[47] There may have been practical concerns. Only church members had the right to vote (and consequently the right to sit on juries),[48] and they were so few in number that it may have been difficult to assemble juries of twelve.[49] But there were almost certainly philosophical concerns as well. The governing law was biblical, and it may have been thought that the necessary expertise to identify and apply that law reposed in the members of the court. To that end, the General Court was specifically empowered to consult the elders of the churches in the jurisdiction.[50] Consultations of this description by lay juries would have been more awkward.

The next thing you would notice, at least in the typical case, is the absence of lawyers. In criminal and civil cases alike, even in capital cases or in cases involving young children, persons appearing before the New Haven courts represented themselves. Representation was not legally prohibited, and as the colony's history progressed, a few persons acting as attorneys appear in the records.[51] But it is unlikely that these were persons with legal training. In a colony populated by believers and traders, persons with legal training were unlikely to be found.

Even when "attorneys" or representatives appeared, they rarely spoke. They simply stood by as the court examined their clients. They never made a legal motion or uttered an objection. In the twenty-four-year history of the colony's trials, not a single motion or objection is to be found.

You would next notice the behavior of the court. Modern lawyers classify judicial styles as either "hot" or "cold." A "hot court" asks lots of questions. A "cold court" listens to legal arguments with the silence of an Easter Island statue. The New Haven courts were most definitely "hot courts." They not only peppered the parties and witnesses with questions but also did not hesitate to volunteer information pertaining to the cases before them.

The questioning process in the New Haven courts was quite unlike that of any court with which we are likely to be familiar. Courts in the English-speaking world ordinarily proceed one witness at a time. Visit a court in Boston or in San Francisco, in London or in Sydney, and the procedure will be the same. A witness will be sworn and questioned by each side. Only when that witness is finished will the next witness be called. The questions will be asked by the lawyers (or, in the absence of lawyers, by the parties). The judge may ask an occasional clarifying question, but by and large, the judge stays out of the fray.

The New Haven courts proceeded differently. Their procedure was much more free flowing and improvisational. The parties and their witnesses appeared together before the court. A claim would be made. The court might begin to hear a witness testify, but before too long, it might ask another witness about what the first witness had just said. Question by question, it would go back and forth between witnesses, sometimes between multiple witnesses. As they heard evidence, the judges would ask the witnesses, in effect, How do you explain this? What do you say about that? Sometimes a witness, a member of the court, or even a spectator would simply pipe up with some new information, and the court would follow up on that as well. In this way, the court could, if all worked well, probe the facts of the case with much greater efficiency than our modern judicial system allows.[52]

You would also notice that the governor, who presided ex officio over both the General Court and the Court of Magistrates, did most of the talking for the tribunal. Although other members of the court occasionally spoke—sometimes to ask a question and sometimes to volunteer information—the governor asked most of the questions and, after the case had been heard, ordinarily delivered the judgment of the court. Whether by reason of status, learning, or force of personality, the governor dominated the court.[53]

Other attributes of the New Haven courts would command your attention as well. One is the courts' frequent reference to pretrial examinations of parties and witnesses. We don't know exactly how the pretrial system worked, but the practice seems to have been that at an early date, a local magistrate (or sometimes the governor himself) would examine a party or witness and memorialize the witness's testimony in a written document that would be transmitted to an upper court for subsequent use at trial. The upper court would then read the document and use it as substantive evidence in the case. Sometimes the pretrial statement of a witness would be used to supplement (or contradict) what the witness later said in court, but often it would be used even if the witness was absent from the proceeding.

This procedure—which permeated the practice of the New Haven courts—had significant implications for both the efficiency and the fairness of the proceedings. The efficiency of the system is obvious. A witness's testimony could be recorded at an early date while his or her memory was fresh and subsequently read by the tribunal without troubling the witness to appear in court. The tribunal could save considerable time as well, since it is much more efficient to read a statement than to question a witness.

What was gained in efficiency, however, was lost in fairness. A witness's credibility cannot always be gauged by reading a piece of paper. Parties appearing in court, often with life or liberty at stake, could not confront their accusers. A famous English case tried in 1603 (that was later, by negative example, to inspire the Confrontation Clause of the Sixth Amendment) provides a troubling example. Sir Walter Raleigh was sent to his death by the deposition testimony of a prosecution witness whom he was unable to confront in court.[54] Had Sir Walter returned from the grave a generation later, he would have recognized the New Haven system all too well.

Viewing the New Haven courts over a period of time, we would also notice a method of decision making quite different from that employed by judges today. Modern judges are expected to be neutral and detached professionals. Their task is to listen to testimony and arguments with open minds and to render judgment only after hearing all of the facts in the case. The New Haven courts had an entirely different view of the judicial task.

Criminal cases began with a presumption of guilt. In practice, this presumption was well nigh conclusive. Toward the end of the colony's history, the Court of Magistrates acquitted a defendant of the crime of which he had been accused. This was such a novel event that the court was at a loss what to do. It felt compelled to find him guilty of something, and it ended up finding him "guilty of suspicion" (see chapter 31, "The Stamford Murder Mystery"). This problem did not, however, frequently arise. Criminal defendants were routinely convicted. The court's task was to question the defendant and confront him with the evidence against him until a confession was forthcoming.

This judicial practice had both practical and ideological roots. In practical terms, the colony's approach was closely connected with the pretrial examination procedure just described. Before a case came to one of the upper courts, a local magistrate would have examined the parties and witnesses shortly after the events in question and written a report of the examination. The members of the upper courts would read the magistrate's report at the beginning of the trial. At least in their own minds, they knew the facts of the case before they had heard the first witness.

Ideology played a role as well. The colony was governed by biblical law. The judges, who consulted with the local clergy, were not wholly secular magistrates. Their task was to execute the law of God, and part of that task was to punish the wicked. Modern notions of judicial neutrality and the presumption of innocence would have been as alien to them as their judicial attitude is to us.

In civil cases—that is, actions for damages between private persons—the situation was somewhat different. Even though, in theory, biblical law was supposed to apply to these cases as well, in these cases applicable biblical law was difficult to identify. While, as we see in "The Piglet's Paternity" in chapter 2, a court could determine the biblical punishment for bestiality by consulting the correct verse in Leviticus, this approach was not available in, for example, a dispute between a merchant and a shoemaker as to who was at fault for a supply of faulty shoes (see chapter 9, "The Faulty Shoes"). As a result, the New Haven courts could be admirably creative in devising solutions to civil disputes, such as assembling a panel of experts in the Case of the Faulty Shoes or engaging in Socratic reasoning with a party in "The Disputed Will" case in chapter 18. The New Haven courts, unfettered by judicial precedent, could be surprisingly progressive in these cases—indeed centuries ahead of their time. The General Court's abandonment of the doctrine of caveat emptor (let the buyer beware) in the Case of the Exploding Gun (chapter 3) and the Court of Magistrates' solicitude for a mistreated apprentice in the Case of the Brickmaker's Apprentice (chapter 26) hold up centuries later as examples of wise and humane judging.

However wrong or even preposterous some of the courts' decisions may seem to modern readers, the trials recounted here are considerably more than a collection of the follies and failures of the past. The New Haven judges were persons of intelligence and learning, working in a differently constructed judicial system and holding a worldview quite different from our own. They, like we, had their professional failures and their professional successes. Modern readers can learn from both.

The People

The New Haven trials are of obvious interest to legal historians, but their importance does not end there. They contain a vivid panorama of the life of the colony. While we read the words of the political and religious leaders of the colony, we also hear a chorus of voices from other strata of society. We hear from pillars of the colony and the church as well as from political and religious dissidents; from merchants and traders; and from rich and poor alike. We hear from persons living in houses staffed with servants and from the servants as well. We hear from farmhands who herd swine and shovel dung. We hear from persons who are gravely injured and persons engaged in grudge matches. We hear from persons who make enemies and persons who fall in love. Importantly, we hear the voices of women and children. Persons of all descriptions appeared before the New Haven courts and had intimate portraits of their lives recorded for posterity.

Reading carefully, we learn that the New Haven Colony, regardless of its official theology, was far from a peaceful assembly of religious folk living quiet lives of biblical virtue. However strict the colony's political and religious rule, turmoil seethed beneath the surface. Church members dissented from the colony's political and religious rule. Women rebelled from the church and its teachings. The colony's young people (no surprise to us!) strayed from its official teachings and had premarital sex. More disturbingly, the colony's economy was built on the labor of women, servants, and children. In scenes that could be drawn from the novels of Dickens, young children were forced into indentured servitude. There are many dark tales in the records, but cases involving the brutal oppression of children are the darkest of all.

This Book

All of these stories (with the exception of redacted sexual matters) appear in the printed records of the nineteenth century, but their original format, even when printed, makes them challenging to read. Contractions, antiquated spellings, and obsolete words abound. Familiarity with the Bible is presumed. Trials are interspersed with the records of legislative and executive business of the colony. Specific trials are sometimes interrupted by other business of the tribunal and must be pieced together from the larger record.

Once the trials are located in the records and the vocabulary and spelling are mastered, the narrative is not always clear. While the records can wonderfully capture the drama of a moment, they can also maddeningly omit key words and phrases in a speech and fail to identify (or occasionally misidentify) the speaker. Sometimes it is difficult to determine who is the person speaking or who is the person being discussed. Every effort has been made to resolve these difficulties, but some problems have proved intractable. Particularly vexing passages are discussed in endnotes accompanying the cases.

The New Haven trials have been previously known and accessible only to a handful of academic specialists. The goal of this book is to make these historic treasures accessible to the general public. To that end, each of the thirty-three cases recounted here is reported in two parts. The first part is a retelling of the case in modernized and intelligible English, with explanatory endnotes where needed. The second part is a commentary on the case.

The aim of the retold cases (indeed the enterprise of the entire book) is to do for the New Haven trials what the great English historian F. W. Maitland hoped to do for the medieval *Year Books*: "to hasten the day when they will once more be readable, intelligible and—we do not fear to say it—enjoyable."[55] The dual aspirations are to modernize the language of the original records and, at the same time, to retain the original's distinctive voice. These are conflicting goals, imperfectly realized. The difficulty is something like that of translating Chaucer into modern English.

No translation will ever do complete justice to the original, but the more readable the modern version is, the more likely it is to depart from the original. The translator strives to retain as much of the original language as possible but with the knowledge that if the original language is simply repeated verbatim, the goal of modernization will be lost.

The titles, headings, introductory material, notes, and commentaries are mine. The notes explain difficult words, phrases, and references. The commentaries discuss the respective trials from a modern legal perspective.

The thirty-three trials recounted here have been culled from a larger number of trials reported in the records. Numerous short trials, briefly stating, for example, that specific persons were convicted of specified crimes or that certain persons were granted divorces or inheritances, are omitted because they shed little light on larger issues. It has also been necessary to omit a number of more lengthy trials because of the exigencies of publication. It is hoped that it will be possible to publish additional trials in the future.

When you read these cases, you will have the satisfaction—and, it is hoped, the pleasure—of discovering a treasure trove of informative and provocative source materials previously known only to a handful of academic specialists. But four cases involving sexual matters occupy an even more rarified category. "The Milford Bestiality Case" (chapter 15), "The Youth Sex Cases" (chapter 17), "The Attempted Bestiality Case" (chapter 22), and "The Lecherous Swineherd" (chapter 32) have never been printed, and the handwritten manuscript that records them has been locked in government vaults for centuries. With the exception of the seventeenth-century secretaries who wrote them and the nineteenth-century librarian who refused to print them, the number of people who have seen these cases must be few indeed. When you read, for example, "The Lecherous Swineherd" (chapter 32), with its Hardyesque tale of a swineherd's seduction of a young servant girl, you will have the excitement of knowing that you are among the first to have read this story in centuries.

The New Haven trials are a great and endlessly interesting heritage. As Maitland said of the *Year Books*, "They come to us from life."[56] It is hoped that this book will enable these endlessly interesting cases to come to life again.

1

꧁꧂

THE

INDIAN'S

NAME

꧁꧂

One day after the New Haven court system was organized, the colony made its first arrest and initiated its first case.[1] This case cannot be fully appreciated without some understanding of the extremely hostile relationship between the European colonists and the Native Americans residing in the area at that time. Between 1634 and 1638, these two groups waged a war known in U.S. history as the Pequot War.

In 1637 an Englishman named Abraham Finch had been killed in Wethersfield, then part of the (separate) Connecticut Colony. A Quinnipiac (the English name for the Renapi, an Algonquin tribe in Connecticut) man named Nepaupuck was accused of his murder. Finch was a casualty of a deadly raid on Wethersfield during the Pequot War. The war had formally ended on September 21, 1638, with the Treaty of Hartford, but tensions remained high among the English and Native populations.[2] The Pequots had lost the war; by the end, about seven hundred Pequots had been killed or taken into captivity. Hundreds of prisoners were sold into slavery in the West Indies. The conflict had embroiled the many tribes in the area including the Niantic, Mohigg, Naragansett, Montauk, and Pequot.

On October 26, 1639, a man calling himself Nepaupuck appeared in New Haven "of his own accord" and, "with a deer's head upon his back," presented himself to New Haven's newly appointed magistrate, Theophilus Eaton. Whether he was, in fact, Nepaupuck was to be the central question in the case. For now, we'll call him the prisoner. The reference to the "deer's head upon his back" is one of the only references to attire in any of the records, so it seems significant—though we don't know whether this detail was to indicate the stature of the man or his difference from the Europeans, or both.

Robert Seely, the colony's newly appointed marshal, made his maiden arrest by apprehending the prisoner on a warrant and tying him up. Seely had been a neighbor of Finch's in Wethersfield and was second in command in the Pequot War. The arrest was anything but routine. Aided by a second Native American, the prisoner attempted to escape. The attempt was unsuccessful. He "was again taken and delivered into the magistrate's power, and . . . kept in the stocks until he might be brought to a due trial." The period of pretrial detention turned out to be a couple of days—short by modern standards but a long time to spend in the stocks, hinged wooden boards that locked his feet in place. In the meantime, Seely's deputy whipped the accomplice who had aided the prisoner.

Two days later, the colony witnessed its first judicial proceeding when the prisoner appeared before the New Haven magistrate and his deputies. The idea seems to have been that the judges would investigate the case and decide whether to refer it to the colony's General Court for trial. In procedural terms, this was roughly analogous to a modern preliminary hearing, in which a court determines whether there is probable cause for a criminal case to proceed to trial. But the proceeding here seems to have had two somewhat different purposes: to examine witnesses and to persuade the prisoner to admit his guilt.

The magistrate and his deputies examined an unspecified number of Indians; their names and tribal affiliations are not given in the record, so we do not know if tribal allegiance motivated them to testify against Nepaupuck or on his behalf. These witnesses told the judges that the prisoner had murdered one or more Englishmen, cut off their hands, and presented the severed hands to a Pequot sachem, "boasting that he had killed them with his own hands."

At this point, a witness intending to help the prisoner entered the room. The witness was the prisoner's kinsman, Mewhebato. As recorded by the court, Mewhebato's testimony did not go well. "At first he pretended ignorance, but with a distracted countenance, and in a trembling manner. Being admonished to speak the truth, he did acknowledge him guilty according to the charge the other Indians had before made."

Now it was the prisoner's turn to testify. The other Indians withdrew, and he was brought in and examined. The question immediately turned to just who he was. He "confessed that Nepaupuck was guilty according to the tenure of the former charge, but denied that he was Nepaupuck."

At this point, Mewhebato was once again brought into the room. After "some signs of sorrow," Mewhebato charged the prisoner "to his face that he had assisted the Pequots in murdering the English. This somewhat abated his spirit and boldness." Another

Indian was brought in and said that he had personally seen the prisoner, whom he called Nepaupuck, murder Abraham Finch in Wethersfield. Finally, the rest of the Indians were brought in. They too said that the prisoner was Nepaupuck and that he had murdered one or more of the English.

At that point, the prisoner, "being by the concurrence of testimony convinced, confessed that he was the man named Nepaupuck." He further "boasted that he was a great captain, had murdered Abraham Finch, and had his hands in other English blood. He said he knew he must die and was not afraid of it, but laid his neck to the mantle-tree[3] of the chimney, desiring that his head might be cut off or that he might die in any other manner that the English should appoint." At this point, he "was returned to the stocks, and as before a watch was appointed for his safe custody."

The General Court met the next day. The trial before this court was more summary than the hearing before the magistrates. The prisoner was "brought to the bar and examined as before." He reverted to his original story. He was not the Nepaupuck who had committed the murder. But, once again, the other "did accuse him to his face." The prisoner then "confessed that he had his hand in the murder of Abraham Finch, but yet he said there was a Mohawk of that name that had killed more than he." At this point, another Indian "affirmed to his face" that the prisoner had killed a number of other men as well. The prisoner was now asked "if he would not confess that he deserved to die." He replied, "It is weregin."

We don't know what "weregin" means; early historians of the New Haven Colony suggest that it means "It is known" or "So be it." The court was satisfied. Having "such pregnant proof," it "proceeded to pass sentence upon him according to the nature of the fact and the rule in that case, he that sheds man's blood, by man shall his blood be shed." The convicted man's head was cut off the next day and pitched upon a pole in the marketplace.

⊰⊱⊰⊱⊰

This brief tale with its bloody conclusion arises from a dramatic clashing of cultures. The opening scene is cinematic and tragic. A seventeenth-century Native American, with his customary religious beliefs and attire, confronts a newly arrived group of European settlers professing the standards of the Bible. The settlers prevail, and the Native American ends up with his severed head pitched on a pole in the settlers' marketplace.

The underlying legal questions raised by this proceeding are equally compelling. By the standards of modern criminal trials, the proceedings here were stunningly inadequate. To begin with the most obvious shortcoming, there was no jury to be found, in spite of the fact that the right to trial by jury had already been established as a cornerstone of English justice for centuries. The "court" had no trained judges. It was, instead, an assemblage of the leaders of the local theocracy, elected to that position a couple of days before and presiding over their maiden case. There were no attorneys. There was not even legal jurisdiction in the modern sense. The murder that was the subject of the trial had occurred in Wethersfield, which was part of the (separate) Connecticut Colony. A modern court, hearing these facts, would simply send the prisoner to the jurisdiction where the crime had been committed.

At first blush, we have something closer to the proverbial judgment of Solomon than to a trial in the modern sense. Everyone knows the story of Solomon and the baby (1 Kings 3:16–28). Two prostitutes each claim to be the mother of an infant. The king hears them out and says, "Bring me a sword." He orders the child divided in two, with half given to each claimant. The false mother thinks this is just fine. The real mother pleads for the child's life. By hearing both sides, without benefit of jury or counsel, the truth becomes manifest.

The judges professed themselves to be biblical men and would doubtless have been flattered by the comparison to Solomon, although it seems what was really at work can be compared to a military tribunal exercising the colony's need to make an example of the accused murderer. Yet there are traces of actual law peeking through the underbrush.

There is biblical law, to start. The punishment meted out is, we are told, expressly dictated by "the rule in that case," namely, "Whoso sheddeth man's blood, by man shall his blood be shed" (Genesis 9:6). This use of biblical law conforms to a resolution adopted by the colony a few months previously that "the Scripture holds forth a perfect rule for the direction and government of all men."

But there are traces of nonbiblical law as well. The court, after all, called itself a "court," and there was plainly an attempt to give both the preliminary proceeding and the ensuing trial some form of legality. The prisoner was arrested on a "warrant," although we don't know who signed the warrant or what it said. There was a formal "charge." The accusers confronted the prisoner "to his face," a privilege famously denied to Sir Walter Raleigh in England earlier in the same century. Each tribunal heard the prisoner speak in person. And the proceedings were officially recorded in notes that we can read today.

What we have is a new form of trial. It isn't the trial by jury mandated by the English law of the time. It's nothing like the elaborate legal proceeding required by modern American law. And it's not a "biblical" trial either. We have instead a newly improvised proceeding created to fit the felt needs of the newly founded colony. As we examine more cases, we'll see how this experiment in legal procedure developed.

2

❧❧❧❧

THE PIGLET'S
PATERNITY

❧❧❧❧

The colony had to wait more than two years before its second
recorded trial occurred, but when it came, it was a doozy.[1] On
February 14, 1642, a planter named John Wakeman informed the
magistrates that a sow he had recently purchased had given birth
to a "prodigious monster." The monster had been born dead, but
Wakeman brought its body for inspection. The dead piglet was
vividly described: "It had no hair on the whole body, the skin was
very tender, and of a reddish white color like a child's. The head
was most strange. It had but one eye in the middle of the face,
and that large and open, like some blemished eye of a man. Over
the eye, in the bottom of the forehead, which was like a child's,
a thing of flesh grew forth and hung down. It was hollow and
like a man's instrument of generation. A nose, mouth, and chin
deformed, but not much unlike a child's. The neck and ears had
also such resemblance."

The most fateful attribute of the dead piglet, however, was a resemblance (or so it was thought) to one George Spencer, formerly
a servant to Henry Browning, the man who had sold the sow to
Wakeman. Spencer, as it happened, had only one good eye. His

other eye was deformed, "and his deformed eye being beheld and compared together with the eye of the monster, seemed to be as like as the eye in the glass to the eye in the face."

Ten days later, on February 24, Spencer was "examined concerning this abomination." He understandably denied paternity of the deformed piglet. The New Haven magistrates, however, committed him to prison "on strong probabilities of this fact." That same evening, one of the magistrates, Stephen Goodyear went to the prison where he found Spencer talking with two other men. Goodyear asked Spencer "if he had not committed that abominable filthiness with the sow." Spencer denied it. Goodyear then asked whether Spencer noticed his likeness in the piglet. Spencer was silent at first but then asked the magistrate whose sow it was. At this, Goodyear apprehended "some relenting" in the prisoner and reminded him of the scriptural admonition "He that hides his sin shall not prosper, but he that confesses and forsakes his sins shall find mercy" (Proverbs 28:13). Goodyear asked Spencer if he wasn't sorry that he had "denied the fact which seemed to be witnessed from heaven against him." At this, Spencer said he was sorry and confessed that he had done it.

The next day, both New Haven magistrates went to the prison "with divers others," urging Spencer to give glory to God and freely confess his sin. Spencer initially denied wrongdoing, but Robert Seely, the marshal, reminded him of his previous confession. At this point, Spencer confessed again. He said that while he was working in Browning's service, "the sow came into the stable, and then the temptation and his corruption did work," whereupon he did the wicked deed.

Spencer was now attracting attention in high places. On February 26, Theophilus Eaton, the governor of the colony, and

John Davenport, the minister of the church, visited Spencer. In the presence of these august persons, Magistrate Goodyear questioned Spencer "more particularly concerning the bestiality, namely how long the temptation had been upon his spirit before he committed it." Spencer answered that "it had been upon his spirit two or three days before." Asked about his prayer habits, he responded that he had not prayed since he came to New England four or five years ago. He said that he had been in the sty with the sow about two hours about six o'clock in the evening, "when the sun was set, and the day light almost shut in."

Following the interview, Spencer was charged "with a profane, atheistical carriage, in unfaithfulness and stubbornness to his master, a course of notorious lying, filthiness, scoffing at the ordinances, ways, and people of God."

The next day, a Sunday, Spencer "caused a bill to be put up, entreating the prayers of the church to God on his behalf, for the pardon of the sins he had committed and confessed."

Three days later, on Wednesday, March 2, Spencer was brought to trial before the General Court. The vague list of charges pending against him was now augmented by a more specific charge: bestiality. The court urged Spencer once again "by confession to give glory to God." Spencer declined to do so. Instead, we are told, "he impudently and with desperate imprecations against himself denied all that he had formerly confessed."

Witnesses were called. Marshal Seely affirmed that Spencer had dictated the Sunday bill asking the prayers of the church "for the pardon of that bestiality." Ezekiel Cheevers affirmed that on Monday, Spencer told him that "the Lord had given him a sight of his sin, and he hoped he would let him see it more." Richard Malbon affirmed that Spencer had "confessed the fact to him." Malbon had helpfully directed Spencer to Leviticus 20:15.[2] Spencer told the marshal that the passage had "struck like a dagger to his heart."

William Harding, a friend of Spencer's, "testified to the prisoner's face in court" that Spencer had told him that "Thomas Badger's sin was worse than his, for Badger lay with a Christian, but himself the prisoner lay but with a rotten sow." Other witnesses testified that Spencer had confessed to them as well.

Spencer was now asked what he had to say for himself. He responded that "the witnesses did him wrong and charged things upon him which he had not spoken." Given this response, the court—although "abundantly satisfied in the evidence"—"began to examine the witnesses upon oath." After four witnesses had confirmed their former testimony "and others were ready to do the like," Spencer "stopped the course." He admitted that he had made the confessions to which the witnesses had testified. But he "obstinately and impudently persisted to deny the fact."

With this evidence before it, the court found Spencer "guilty of this unnatural and abominable crime of bestiality, and that he was acted by a lying spirit in his denials." By the "rule" of Leviticus 20:15, both the prisoner and the sow were sentenced to death.

The execution was not carried out immediately. Instead, the court ordered the time of execution and the kind of death to be delayed until the next General Court. In the meantime, the New Haven authorities wrote to Massachusetts and other places for advice as to what should be done with the prisoner.[3]

The chronology in the records is confusing, but it appears that the next General Court met on April 2.[4] Spencer was once again brought forth blinking from the prison to face the tribunal. The court "demanded whether he would yet give glory to God in owning his guilt in that loathsome sin of bestiality." Spencer, however, "retained his former obstinacy" and "peremptorily denied it." At this point, two of the witnesses in Spencer's original trial "gave in evidence in court to his face" that, after his sentencing, Spencer "had fully confessed the fact to them." After hearing these witnesses, Spencer acknowledged his confessions. When asked why he continued to deny the crime, he answered it was "because he neither knew heaven nor hell." Two additional witnesses then testified that Spencer had given postsentence confessions to them.

The court "demanded" whether Spencer "would yet give glory to God in a free acknowledgment of his sinful and abominable filthiness in the bestiality." Spencer responded that "he would leave it to God, adding that he had condemned himself by his former confessions." The court found itself "abundantly satisfied" of Spencer's guilt and the correctness of his sentence. It ordered that Spencer should be hanged "but that first the forementioned sow at the said place of execution shall be slain in his sight, being run through with a sword."

This terrible sentence was carried out on April 8, 1642. In then traditional English fashion, Spencer was brought to the place of execution on a cart and allowed to deliver a gallows address to the waiting crowd. "After some pause, he began to speak to the youths about him, exhorting them all to take warning by his example how they neglect and despise the means of Grace, and their soul's good, as he had done." He was once again urged to acknowledge his crime, and he once again denied it. But when the halter was fitted to his neck, "he fully confessed the bestiality in all the circumstances." Though "much pressed," he would not speak further of his sin. With this, the sentence was carried out on Spencer and the sow, "leaving him a terrible example of divine justice and wrath."

ఞ౸ఞ

This horrifying case is a sad reflection on the credulity of mankind and the shortcomings of a legal system that had jettisoned any pretense of fairness to the accused.

Some traces of legality remained. The vague charges of bad character originally levied against Spencer were augmented (albeit at the outset of the trial) by the more specific charge of bestiality. The witnesses in the case testified in the presence of the accused. Spencer was allowed to speak in person to the tribunal deciding his fate, although that tribunal had little interest in hearing anything from him other than a confession. The sentence was decided according to a "rule" of (biblical) law. And there was a record of the proceeding.

Both the process and the outcome, however, bear little resemblance either to modern notions of justice or even to contemporaneous notions of English justice. As in the trial of Nepaupuck, there were no jurors or attorneys to be found. Once again, a high premium is placed on confession by the accused. But the preliminary hearing before a tribunal of magistrates that we saw in the trial of Nepaupuck has disappeared. The magistrates now visited the prison and, joined by the marshal, browbeat the prisoner into confessing.

The record of Spencer's trial is of particular legal interest for the light it sheds on the use of the oath. The testimony originally given against Spencer was unsworn. After Spencer had heard this testimony and denied it, the witnesses were sworn and testified again, this time under oath. This practice stands in contrast to long-standing tenets of English law, requiring prosecution (although not defense) witnesses to be sworn. Perhaps due to the admonition of Matthew 5:34 and the memory of English legal repression directed against them, the early Puritan colonists were reluctant to use oaths.[5] It appears that oaths were used only as a last resort, in cases where attempts to obtain a full judicial confession from the accused had failed.

3

⟨⟨⟨⟨⟨⟩⟩⟩⟩⟩

THE

EXPLODING

GUN

⟨⟨⟨⟨⟨⟩⟩⟩⟩⟩

Three years after the execution of George Spencer, the New Haven court considered a civil case.[1] Although the participants would not have recognized the term, we would call it a product liability action.

In December 1645, Stephen Medcalfe appeared before the General Court and told the following story. When he was in the house of one John Linley, John's brother, Francis Linley, had offered to sell him a gun. Medcalfe asked if it was a good one, and Francis answered, "Yea, as any was in the town." The parties agreed on a price of seventeen shillings.

As Medcalfe was leaving, he questioned the sufficiency of the lock mechanism. Francis admitted that John Nash, the local blacksmith, had told him "she was not worth three pence," but he added that Nash had also disparaged another gun that was "a good one for all that."

Nash apparently knew more than Francis had let on. When Medcalfe went home with the gun and fired it, the breech (the end of the barrel) flew out and struck his eye, seriously wounding him. Medcalfe now wanted damages from Francis.

Francis responded that he had duly informed Medcalfe of Nash's opinion. He added that he had also told Medcalfe that the barrel was thin and would not bear a new breech. He said that he had advised Medcalfe to scour the gun well "and if he tried her, to put but a little charge in her."

Unfortunately for Francis, he had previously been examined before Thomas Gregson, a New Haven magistrate, and his story at the trial was not consistent with what he had told Gregson. (We don't know exactly what form this examination took, but it sounds like something more formal than a chance conversation.) The magistrate told the court that Francis had denied telling Medcalfe that the barrel was thin and would not bear a new breech.

Nash followed Magistrate Gregson. Nash testified that he had told Francis "it was a very naughty piece, not worth the mending." He further told Francis that "the barrel at the breech was as thin as a shilling, cracked from the breech to the touch-hole and would not bear a breech." Notwithstanding this advice, Francis told Nash to mend the firearm as well as he could. After he had mended it, Nash told Francis that he would not give three pence for it and "he would not discharge it for all New Haven, for it would do some mischief."

Richard Myles testified that he had overheard Nash tell Francis of the gun's "badness and unserviceableness."

The focus of the trial finally turned to Francis's brother, John Linley. John was asked "why he was taken with such a quaking and trembling" when Medcalfe was about to shoot. John denied any quaking or trembling. Thomas Clark testified about a conversation with John: John had told Clark that when he heard

Medcalfe discharge the gun, John was afraid Medcalfe had hurt himself. The wonderfully named Goodwife Fancy testified that John had visited Medcalfe on what John thought was Medcalfe's deathbed "to know if he would clear his brother, for he said he feared he had hard thoughts of his brother concerning the gun." Thomas Pell, who had apparently acted as Medcalfe's physician, confirmed this testimony. Pell added that Medcalfe's medical expenses amounted to ten pounds.

The court considered this testimony and ordered Francis Linley to pay Medcalfe twenty pounds in damages.[2] It based the size of this award on the loss of Medcalfe's eye, the loss of his time, and "the great charge of the cure."

⋄⋄⋄⋄⋄

While the Case of the Piglet's Paternity shows the New Haven court at its medieval worst, the Case of the Exploding Gun shows the court as, at least in some ways, a surprisingly modern institution. It is true that neither jurors or attorneys are anywhere to be seen. But the court went to great pains to hear both the parties and all the relevant witnesses and delivered a judgment that seems reasonable and compassionate, given the limited information we have about the extent of Medcalfe's injuries.

The procedure used by the parties in this case was miles away from the centuries-old system of common-law pleading used in English (and most American) courts until well into the nineteenth century. Had Medcalfe brought his case in England, he would have had to employ an attorney to draft an exceptionally complicated written pleading setting forth all of the facts legally relevant to his cause of action. A failure to do this correctly would be fatal to his cause. Similarly, his opponent would have had to hire an attorney to attempt to find fault with the first pleading and to draft a responsive pleading of his own. (As we'll see in a moment, under contemporary English law, any action brought by Medcalfe would have had plenty of legal faults to find.) In some cases, the parties could keep trading replies and surreplies for quite some time, all the while arguing the technical defects of their opponents' legal handiwork. In *Medcalfe v. Linley*, however, this complicated pleading process was simply skipped over. It looks as if there was some rudimentary form of pretrial discovery, since Magistrate Gregson had examined Francis Linley prior to the trial. But the parties were not judged on their pleadings. They could simply appear before the court and tell their sides of the story.

The trial was also surprisingly modern in terms of substantive law. Perhaps because this was a civil case, there was no citation to the Old Testament. The court may have attempted to act in a Solomonic way, but its judgment was not burdened with either biblical or contemporaneous legal precedent.

It's a good thing for Medcalfe that this was so. English law at the time was decisively caveat emptor (let the buyer beware). A famous English legal case at the time illustrates the point. In 1603, a man named Chandelor purchased what he thought was a precious stone from a London goldsmith. The goldsmith told Chandelor the stone was a "bezar-stone,"[3] and Chandelor paid the enormous sum of one hundred pounds to buy it. In reality, the stone was a fake. Chandelor sued the goldsmith and won an award in an English trial court. The goldsmith took an appeal, however, and succeeded in overturning the verdict. The justices held that there could be no cause of action against the goldsmith for "the bare affirmation" that it was a bezar-stone. This was the case even if the goldsmith actually knew it wasn't a bezar-stone all along. The court reasoned that "everyone in selling his wares will affirm that his wares are good, or the horse which he sells is sound." A cause of action only exists if the seller "warrants" that the goods are what they purport to be.[4]

Francis Linley hadn't "warranted" his gun to be safe. If Medcalfe had brought his case before an English court, with an attorney and the right to jury trial, he would have been out of luck. From a modern point of view, the Solomonic decision of the General Court was infinitely more fair.

4

❦

THE

"BILLINGSGATE

SLUT"

❦

On the same day (December 3, 1645) that the General Court heard the Case of the Exploding Gun, it heard an action of a different sort brought by Hannah Marsh.[1] Marsh's case was what we would now call a defamation case, although, unlike the modern lawsuit, it was not an action for damages. As we'll see, the court addressed the matter with the outward procedure of a lawsuit but, true to the court's religious character, ended up resolving the matter as an internal church affair.

Marsh complained to the court that Francis Brewster had called her a "Billingsgate slut"[2] and had additionally said that she had been "sent for on shipboard to play the slut."

Brewster did not contest using the words complained of. In fact, he added a few more of his own for good measure, saying, "He hoped she would dance about the whipping post." His defense was that the words were justified. He had been "much provoked and disquieted" by Marsh's "frowardness and brawling on shipboard."[3] Brewster affirmed that one Mrs. Norton of Charlestown told him that "a seaman was speaking filthy words" to Marsh and asked her to go on shipboard "to play the slut."

Brewster's defense was corroborated by the testimony of other witnesses. George Walker testified that he had also heard Mrs. Norton's remarks. Two maids, one employed by Brewster and another employed by a member of the court named George Lamberton, testified that Marsh "was very froward and contentious and a cause of much contention and unquietness amongst them as they came from the Bay."

Governor Theophilus Eaton, presiding over the court, stated what he understood to be the ordinary meaning of the term "Billingsgate slut." "Some that were so called," he told the court, "were convicted scolds and punished at the cucking stool for it, and some of them charged with incontinency."[4]

Given this helpful definition, Brewster responded that he "had sufficiently proved the one true and he would not acquit her in the other." When asked his ground for this "implicit charge," he said that he relied solely on Mrs. Norton's words.

The court had heard enough. In its view, both parties had engaged in deplorable behavior. The court told Brewster that "he ought to acknowledge his failing and so repair her reputation as much as he may." Brewster acknowledged that he was to blame in the matter and said that he was sorry he had spoken so rashly and that "he intended no such charge against her."

The court then turned to Marsh and reproved her "for her froward disposition," reminding her that "meekness is a choice ornament for women and wished her to take it as a rebuke from God and to keep a better watch over her spirit hereafter, lest the Lord proceed to manifest his displeasure further against her."

Marsh acknowledged "it had been some trouble to her that she had been so froward and contentious to the disquieting of others and hoped it should be a warning to her for time to come."

❧

The "Billingsgate Slut" Case says much about the expected deportment of women in the New Haven Colony (and how expected deportment may have differed from actual deportment), but it also gives us a valuable insight into the General Court's view of the proper handling of defamation cases. As mentioned, the court seems to have handled the case as an internal church matter. Both parties were reprimanded for their behavior—Marsh "for her froward disposition" and Brewster for maligning Marsh's reputation. Both parties acknowledged blame and assured the court that they would try to improve their behavior in the future. A somewhat censorious pastor conducting a joint counseling session could not hope for a better result.

It doesn't appear that Marsh wanted (or could reasonably have expected) monetary damages in the first place. She simply complained to the court about the words Brewster had used to describe her. Raymond Donovan, the secretary of labor under President Reagan, famously asked, after being acquitted of fraud, "Where do I go to get my reputation back?" Marsh, it appears, wanted her reputation back. Although the court proceeding could hardly have enhanced her reputation, she did receive something approaching an apology from Brewster at the end of the process. Whether she was satisfied with the decidedly mixed result of the case is unknowable.

As it happens, the court's treatment of Marsh's complaint as an intrachurch matter was consistent with the way English courts had viewed such matters for hundreds of years. Defamation lawsuits in England had been administered in ecclesiastical courts since the thirteenth century. Medieval church law called for the excommunication of persons uttering defamatory remarks. Complainants came to the ecclesiastical courts seeking not damages but penance. But in practice some accommodation between the parties often resulted from the process. Under canon law, doing penance usually involved making suitable amends to the person affronted.[5] Whether this involved the exchange of apologies or the exchange of money would depend on the situation. Although the royal courts slowly began to offer the remedy of monetary damages in some defamation cases, the ecclesiastical courts continued to exercise jurisdiction over cases involving allegations of sexual misconduct well into the seventeenth century. In England, as well as New Haven, these matters were viewed as internal church affairs.[6]

Unlike contemporary English courts, whether ecclesiastical or royal, the General Court required no complicated pleading for a complainant to obtain a hearing. Marsh simply appeared before the court and stated her case. The matter was resolved on the spot, with reprimands to both parties. Whatever one thinks of the substance of its ruling, the ruling was made with admirable efficiency.

5

❧

NEW HAVEN'S
WATERGATE

❧

We are, the psalmist tells us, conceived in iniquity and born in guilt (Psalm 51:5).[1] Every society has its share of saints and sinners. Every so often, someone supposed to be a saint turns out to be a sinner instead. Such was the case with Thomas Fugill, pillar of the church and falsifier of records.

Fugill was one of the founders of the colony and quickly moved into positions of leadership. He was the secretary of the colony. The earliest New Haven records are actually in his handwriting. Soon after John Davenport was named pastor of the church, Fugill was named one of the church's "seven pillars." Given his important role in the colony, he would have been entitled to a prime division of land in the original settlement. Later, in 1641, the colony awarded him a "second division" of land near West Rock, on the outskirts of the settlement.

According to the official record of 1641, the specification of Fugill's "second division" was generous. The record states (the exact wording would come to be important) that "Fugill is allowed his second division at the foot of the West Rock of the clear ground which is there, or so much of it as he desires, according to his proportion." As we'll see, Fugill desired quite a bit. He could certainly rely on the official record. That record had been personally written by the secretary of the colony—none other than Thomas Fugill.

Fast forward to 1646. Perhaps suspecting that something was amiss, the General Court ordered another of the original settlers, John Brocket, to visit Fugill's second division and measure it. Brocket reported back that he had surveyed the land and found that, while Fugill's "full proportion" of land in that area was twenty-four acres, Fugill had instead taken over fifty-two acres.

The court was not pleased. It asked Fugill "what warrant or ground" he had for doing what he had done. Fugill confessed his fault in fencing in the land without a surveyor and "his sinful miscarriage in taking in a quantity so far above his proportion."

The court found this worthy of censure, but there was more to come. It turned out that the 1641 record had been falsified. The actual grant to Fugill had specified that his second division had to be more than two miles from the center of town, not granted to any other person, and bordered by two rivers in the area. Fugill's official notes had left out both the two-mile limit and the reference to the rivers. Instead, his notes had added the clause "or so much as he desires."

There was still more. Fugill had kept at least *three* sets of books. It appears that none of these books agreed with each other. Two of the books left out the clause "not granted to any other person." All of them had added the clause "or so much as he desires."

The local schoolmaster, Ezekiel Cheevers, decided to inspect more carefully the official record that Fugill had written down in 1641. When the book was viewed, it appeared that the clause "according to his proportion" was itself a late insertion, added "with other pen and ink, a less character and crooked, as with a trembling hand." Cheevers proceeded to question Fugill about this matter "before the Governor and elders." When Fugill began to justify himself, the governor stepped in.

"To prevent further rashness and sinful expression," the governor cautioned Fugill that the book was within and he had viewed it. If the governor could judge the writing, "these words were added and written after the former part of the order with other pen and ink and with a different character." When Fugill boldly offered to take an oath to the contrary, the book was brought out. The difference in the handwriting was so apparent that Fugill changed his story.

Fugill now said that he would take an oath that he had not written in the book after Cheevers had seen and reviewed it. At this point, Fugill's second book was sent for and examined by the governor and elders. That book contained a similar addition, apparently in different handwriting, although a line drawn in blacker ink made the difference in handwriting difficult to discern.

The governor then told the court that he had privately warned Fugill that his protests and offers to take an oath were "bold and sinful." In the governor's view, "confident contradictions" would not "drive men from the truth they knew." Moreover, as the governor saw it, "Oaths, even in certain truths, are not lawful until they are necessary and duly called for." Instead, he reminded Fugill of the "rule" to "let your communication be yea, yea, nay, nay." The governor explained that "profane men indeed in other places who little attend truth think they must swear that they may be believed, and in his [Fugill's] place, it would be no other than a high breach of the third commandment."

Fugill attempted to justify his taking the oath, but when reminded of the particular facts before the court, he "began again to turn and wind and so to evade the governor's testimony but gave no satisfaction."

Hearing this, some of the members of the court suggested it might be appropriate to choose another secretary of the colony. Fugill "confessed his unfitness for the place by reason of a low voice, a dull ear, and slow apprehensions." The court told him that it "had long taken notice of sundry miscarriages through weakness or neglect, yet in tender respect to himself and his family, they had continued him in the place." This, however, was the last straw. "They were called to lay aside these private respects for the public safety." Fugill was promptly voted out of office.

Fugill's troubles had not ended. Four months later, he appeared before the court to be sentenced "for his unrighteousness in taking and detaining of the town's land and falsifying of orders." Fugill pleaded that he had already lost his position as secretary of the colony and, in addition, the church had excommunicated him. He also pleaded that he had suffered great "bodily weakness." The court, however, found further punishment appropriate. He was ordered to pay a fine of twenty pounds to the town. In addition, his land was "reduced to its due bounds, according to the first grant, namely between the two rivers and without the two miles."

⋙⋘

The trial of Thomas Fugill was surely an odd sort of trial not only by modern standards but also by sixteenth-century standards. Rather than being a formal trial commenced by some sort of official charge or accusation, the proceeding began as an investigation into the size of Fugill's acreage and quickly metamorphosed into a trial concerning the falsification of records. Once again, of course, there were no jurors or attorneys to be found. The governor's reprimand of Fugill for his willingness to take an oath underlines the cultural aversion that the New Haven court had to oath taking in general. Instead, we are told, the court (or at least the governor) wanted unsworn witnesses simply to say "yea, yea, nay, nay."

This being said, some features of Fugill's trial strike a familiar chord to the modern observer. The close scrutiny of the handwriting and ink used in the allegedly altered document is vaguely reminiscent of modern handwriting analysis, although it is striking that no one thought to compare the handwriting in question to known exemplars of Fugill's handwriting. This is the first thing that a modern handwriting expert would do and wouldn't have been difficult for the New Haven court, since many of its own records had been written by Fugill himself.

Beyond the particulars of the handwriting and the oaths, however, some universal truths, known to observers of trials in every age, peek through this little narrative. It's never a good idea to change your story during a trial, and witnesses who do this (there are many) invariably make a poor impression. Ditto for the witness who begins to "turn and wind and so to evade" the questions, as Fugill did when examined by the governor. Needless to say, it's not a good idea to keep two sets of books. Keeping three sets of books is surely beyond the pale. Above all, physical evidence prevails over oral testimony. Fugill could hardly deny the physical dimensions of his landholdings. And whatever he said by way of explanation, he could not overcome the physical facts of different handwriting and different ink.

6

❧❧❧

THE SEXUAL
HARASSMENT CASE

❧❧❧

Sexual harassment in the workplace is a focal point of modern employment law and a source of periodic headline news when the perpetrators turn out to be public figures, but there is nothing new under the sun.[1] The travails of Goodwife Fancy (whom we briefly met as a witness in the Case of the Exploding Gun) stand as eloquent testimony to the appalling workplace conditions faced by countless low-status women in every age, including our own. Although her voice was heard, her ultimate fate stands as an indictment of the General Court.

In April 1646, Governor Theophilus Eaton, "being informed of several lewd passages, ordered William Fancy to appear with his wife at the court to answer for them." At some point, both spouses were examined outside of court, and their examinations were subsequently read in court.

Goodwife Fancy (we never learn her first name) told the examiner that, about two years previously, she had been working for Goodwife Robinson. She found herself alone in a cellar with Goodwife Robinson's husband, Thomas Robinson. Thomas took hold of her, pulled down his breeches, put his hand under her skirt,[2] and "with strength and force labored to satisfy his lust and to defile her." When she cried out, he covered her mouth. He finally left when he heard some shipmen calling him.

Later, when the Fancys were living in the cellar of Robert Seely, a lieutenant in the artillery company, she went out in a cornfield to bring in a barrow of wood. She heard a noise in the cornstalks and, looking about, saw Thomas Robinson. She told him, "Go and be hanged. What do you here?" Robinson, however, "fastened upon her [and] strove to have kissed her." When she cried out, he left her.

Another time, Goodwife Robinson sent her out to gather pumpkins. Thomas Robinson made a similar attempt, but she resisted and told him that "these practices of his would not long be hid."

Again, when she was attempting to catch a hen, Thomas Robinson "came and put down his breeches [and] strove to stop her mouth." Goodwife Fancy made a noise, and her husband came out of the cellar. Seeing her husband, Robinson left.

Later, about a year before the trial, the Fancys lived at the house of Thomas Clark. Goodwife Fancy saw Robinson coming and "fearing his filthy lustful attempts, got and stayed out of the house." Robinson prayed her to come in, but Goodwife Fancy told him that since "her husband knew of his filthy lewd carriages, he must therefore make peace with him."

Several weeks before the trial, Thomas Robinson called on William Fancy and told him that Goodwife Robinson wanted "help in her childbed state." Fancy, "considering the woman's need," obligingly consented to allow his wife to provide the requested assistance. Things went well for a week, but in the second week Robinson "returned to his former filthy course." Goodwife Fancy went with Robinson to the cowhouse one evening to hold a lantern while he caught a hen. Suddenly, Robinson darkened the lantern and "took hold of her in the dark." She cried out, "What shall I do?" Robinson "put down his breeches, put his hands under her skirt, and got them up, thrust her to the wall . . . and endeavored with his body to commit adultery with her." Goodwife Fancy resisted and told him that if he continued "he would come to the gallows." Robinson "pished at that, but told her he would never meddle with her more."

Needless to say, this wasn't the end of things. Later, Goodwife Fancy went out to fetch wood for a fire. "Robinson followed her, put down his breeches, and endeavored to satisfy his lust as before." She cried out and threatened to tell his wife. Robinson desisted and assured her that this was his "last attempt upon her."

Goodwife Fancy told her examiner that she had "acquainted her husband with Robinson's lewd, lustful attempts upon her" (except for the cowhouse incident, which happened at a later time) and "pressed him to complain to the Governor." Her husband, however, refused, saying that his wife, having been previously convicted of thievery,[3] would not be believed.

Robinson's harassment of Goodwife Fancy eventually came to light as a result of her larcenous past. Robinson, hearing that a pair of scissors was missing, told some people that he thought he had seen the scissors at Goodwife Fancy's home and that she was a thief. Goodwife Fancy learned of this allegation through one of her employers, Goodwife Thomas. She responded with a proverb: "Save one from the gallows and he will hang you or cut your throat if he can." When Goodwife Thomas inquired what this meant, Goodwife Fancy disclosed her history of abuse.

Once Goodwife Fancy had spilled the beans and Robinson's wife found out about it, Robinson became repentant. Weeping passionately, he met Goodwife Fancy at the cutler's shop and told her, "He would rather that his life and all goods were gone than that his wife should have known of it."

Neither Robinson nor Goodwife Fancy wanted the case to go public, but Goodwife Thomas insisted on seeing some "general reformation" in Robinson's conduct. Robinson met with one Robert Usher that night and said that his previous remarks were "but a word in jest" and that William Fancy's wife had wronged him. These statements provoked Usher rather than satisfying him, and "it was resolved that counsel should be asked and proceeding ordered accordingly."

Robinson was desperate to settle the matter. About two weeks before the trial, he offered the Fancys ten shillings in silver to drop the prosecution. The Fancys apparently declined the offer and testified in court that it had been made.

John Thomas and his wife testified that Robinson had acknowledged "some miscarriages" to them and "did weakly if at all deny the rest" of Goodwife Fancy's charges. Robinson also told them that he knew "that a woman's word would pass before a man's in this case."

Thomas Robinson's wife told the court that her husband had confessed that "he had spoken some words to try Fancy's wife, but he could not own all she had charged him with." Hearing this, the court asked her where her husband was now. She dramatically replied that "yesterday, in the afternoon, he went forth in a sad discontented frame, and as she since heareth, passed over the ferry, but since she hath not heard of him."

With this dramatic announcement, the case against Thomas Robinson ended. As far as the New Haven Colony records indicate, he was never seen again.[4]

Robinson's disappearance was not, however, the end of the

court's inquiry into sexual matters involving Goodwife Fancy. William Fancy further testified that, about three months previously, one Mark Meggs had come to their house to collect a debt of eight shillings and asked for him. As Goodwife Fancy passed by him, Meggs "caught hold of her, put his hand under her skirt, showed her a string of wampum [beads], and told her he would give her that and five shillings more if she would teach him to get [beget] a boy." When Goodwife Fancy resisted, Meggs went away. She told her husband what Meggs had done, whereupon Mr. Fancy and the cutler went to speak to him. Meggs acknowledged his fault to them and, later, to Goodwife Fancy.

The "cutler," it turns out, was none other than Stephen Medcalfe, whom we earlier met when his eye was injured by a defective gun. Regardless of the state of his eyesight, Medcalfe apparently remained vigorous in other ways. Shortly after the gun accident, the Fancys were staying in Medcalfe's house. While Goodwife Fancy was sifting meal, Medcalfe came "in a base, lustful way to kiss her by force." She told him, "It were better he never touched any while he lived." One night, when William Fancy was away, Medcalfe entered her room, frightening her, but went away when she cried out. She told her husband when he returned, but her husband dissuaded her from complaining to the magistrate.

The court now turned to Mark Meggs. Meggs denied Goodwife Fancy's charge, but William Fancy testified that Meggs had told him if the matter "came to light he should be undone."

John Mosse, a corporal of the local militia, informed the court of what one James Heywood had told him: "Mark Meggs came into Goody Fancy's house, and down with his breeches." Another witness, Goodman Bannister, testified of what William Fancy had told him: "Robinson was run away and feared his wife would be a cause of his being whipped and so Mark Meggs."

Mark Meggs's brother, John Meggs, informed the court that William Fancy had told him what his brother Mark had done and that he thought his brother would be fined.

John Thomas then said that Mark Meggs had attempted to dissuade him from coming to court by falsely telling him the governor had said his attendance would not be required.

Robert Usher informed the court that Mark Meggs had asked to meet with the Fancys and that Goodwife Fancy had declined to tell him what the meeting was about.

Goodwife Fancy now testified under oath. She told the court that Mark Meggs had come to her house to collect a debt of eight or ten shillings. He caught hold of her, put his hands under her skirt, offered her a string of wampum, and said that he had five shillings more if she would teach him to get a boy.

William Fancy was also placed under oath. He testified that Mark Meggs had "met him, acknowledged his fault, and said if he should go and tell of it he should be undone."

Captain Daniel How, a member of the court, now addressed Mark Meggs directly. "It was not his way," How told Meggs, "to deny it before God and a court of justice, for though the court might, God would not clear him if guilty, for God may have left him to the act, although there may want evidence, as he may remember a defect of evidence in a case of this nature formerly." Therefore, How "desired him not to leave God and himself in this act."

Unmoved by this exhortation, Meggs continued to deny the allegation. How's concern that the court might clear Meggs even if he was guilty turned out to be misplaced. For his "sinful and lustful attempt," Meggs was sentenced "to be severely whipped."

To make justice complete, in the eyes of the court, each of the Fancys then received the same sentence meted out to Meggs.

Goodwife Fancy, for "concealment of the forementioned villainous and lustful attempts by several as appears by her own confessions," and William Fancy, "for his being as it were a pander to his wife and neglecting the timely revealing of these forementioned attempts to have defiled his wife," were each sentenced "to be severely whipped."

⟡⟡⟡⟡

Reading this travesty of a case, the modern reader cannot help but despair at the human condition. No matter how society, government, and the law might change, the same familiar drama occurs in everyday life from age to age. A low-status woman goes out in the world to work in a menial job in order to put food on the table, and her reward is to be groped and harassed at every turn. We see this happen on a regular basis today.

The poignancy of Goodwife Fancy's story arises from its ordinariness. The scribe of the trial, who vividly brings so many salient details to light, doesn't even dignify her with a first name. She and her husband are among the lowest of the low. They live in the cellars of various houses (they seem to move from time to time), and she does menial work in the fields and kitchen for the wives of more prosperous settlers. Whether she goes out in the field or stays at home, she is never safe. Men grope her and abuse her at every opportunity. With what turns out to be good reason, her husband tells her not to go to the authorities. Even if she does go to the authorities, she is told that no one will believe her because she has a criminal record. When someone else, at long last, tells the authorities what is going on, her principal abuser flees the jurisdiction unpunished, and she and her husband are the ones sentenced to be severely whipped.

Perhaps the one ray of light in this gloomy picture is that, when her accusations were ultimately heard in court, Goodwife Fancy's story *was* believed. Although Thomas Robinson had removed himself from the jurisdiction, Mark Meggs remained before the court. The court heard both Goodwife Fancy's accusation and Meggs's denial. But it heard the testimony of other witnesses as well and concluded on the evidence that Meggs had indeed made a "sinful and lustful attempt." Whether Goodwife Fancy was comforted during her whipping by the thought that Meggs had received the same punishment is dubious in the extreme.

7

❧❧❧

THE WOMEN

DISSIDENTS

❧❧❧

The 1646 trial of three women for "several miscarriages of a public nature" reveals the Orwellian nature of life in the New Haven Colony.[1] The community was centered on the church, and the word of the minister was law. Dissent was not permitted. Potential informants were everywhere. Any person so bold as to question the minister risked being brought before the General Court. This was the unhappy experience of Mrs. Brewster, Mrs. Moore, and Mrs. Leach.[2]

As readers of Victorian novels will recognize, servants could hear many things said in a house. Once a servant left her position, there was little to stop her from relating what she had heard. This was the case with Elizabeth Smith, "late servant to Mrs. Leach," who informed the court what she had heard in her former service.

One day, Smith told the court, she heard Mrs. Brewster "loud in conference" with Mrs. Eaton,[3] Mrs. Moore, and Mrs. Leach "as she sat at work in the next room." Apparently finding the "conference" to be of interest, Smith called a fellow servant, Job Hall, to listen with her because he "could better remember the particulars of such a conference than herself." Hall later joined Smith in testifying before the court.

The servants had a great deal to say. Their charges against Brewster alone are divided by the records into twelve different allegations, much like a modern-day bill of particulars (a legal list of charges). The court heard each of these charges, allowing Brewster to respond at each turn. None of these replies proved persuasive to the court. Here are the twelve charges made by Smith and Hall.

First, Brewster had discussed a sermon given by John Davenport, minister of the church. Although Hall—who had been recruited for his ostensibly superior memory—"was somewhat doubtful" as to who exactly said what, he implied that Brewster had criticized Davenport for saying that persons "could not have salvation without coming into the church."

Brewster denied the charge. This, apparently, repeated an earlier denial that she had made to the governor and the magistrate.

Second, Brewster had disputed a comment that Davenport had made in a sermon on Ephesians 4:12.[4] Davenport had said, "If a man lived where he might join the church and did not, it would prove a delusion to him." Brewster stated that when she heard these words, "her stomach wombled as when she bred [a] child." According to Smith, Brewster said she was "sermon sick" two or three times and, when she came home, told her son to "make waste paper" of her notes of Davenport's sermon.

Brewster denied using these words but admitted saying that "her stomach wrought, smelling an ill savor in the seat." Her explanation, we are told, "gave no satisfaction to the court."

Third, Brewster asked Moore "whether she had not heard for

what Mrs. Eaton was cast out of the church."[5] Moore asked Eaton why she did not confess her sin. Eaton replied that she had done so but not to the church's satisfaction. Brewster said that "if Mrs. Eaton had seen her light before she came into the church, she had not come in."

Brewster said she didn't remember speaking the words in question, but she had "heard that Mrs. Eaton came into the church in a hurry and went out in a hurry."

Fourth, Brewster said that making "contributions" at the church "was as going to mass or going up to the high altar." (The congregants apparently brought their offerings to the altar during church services.) When Moore asked her why she went to them, Brewster answered that she went because her husband had commanded her to do so.

Brewster denied using these words. According to her, Moore asked "what rule there was for going to the high altar in the contributions," and Eaton had "defended the practice of the church."

Fifth, Brewster said that Thomas Fugill (whom we met in his trial for falsifying orders) confided to her a scandalous statement of Governor Theophilus Eaton. Unhappily, we don't know what the scandalous statement was. Brewster had suggested to Fugill that "they go two and two together and writer down what scandalous persons say and compare their writings." This was necessary because if "they" find any contradictions, she and Fugill would be charged with lying. She concluded, "I pray God keep me from them." Brewster denied all of this.

Sixth, Brewster asked Leach whether she had any mind to join the church, and Leach had answered no. Brewster responded that "your mother [Mrs. Moore] is a woman of wisdom. She can teach you well enough at home." Brewster denied saying this.

Seventh, when Moore asked Brewster "whether she saw the persons whipped for their unnatural filthiness about a month since," Brewster said, "No, but they were cruelly whipped, and her son said he had rather fall into the hands of the Turks and hath rather be hanged than fall into their hands."

Brewster not only denied speaking of cruelty in the punishment in question but also said, "She rather thought they deserved more." She had not heard her son speak of falling into the hands of the Turks, but he did say that "if he were fit for death, he would rather be hanged than so whipped."

Eighth, Brewster told Moore "in a scoffing manner" of an encounter "with some sister of the church" in which they had discussed the pending expulsion from the church of one William Preston.

Brewster admitted the conversation, identifying the "sister" as Goodie Charles, but denied the scoffing. Hall and Smith replied by saying that Brewster "used to laugh and scoff at all the former passages they have respectively testified."

Ninth, Brewster said loudly to Mrs. Eaton that "they could not banish her but by a General Court, and if it came to that, she wished Mrs. Eaton to come to her and acquaint her with her judgment and grounds about baptizing."[6] Mrs. Brewster would then "seduce some other woman." Brewster, Eaton, and the other woman would then each complain of the other, and "so they would be banished together," perhaps going to Rhode Island.

Brewster confessed to this charge but claimed her words had been spoken in jest.

Tenth, Brewster loudly told Hall that "she would have you and your harlot to the whipping post."

Brewster, Moore, and Leach acknowledged that Brewster had

used these words but argued that the "harlot" reference was directed to Smith, rather than someone more intimately associated with Hall.

Eleventh, on the same day that Brewster talked to Hall, she called Smith a liar and a "brazen faced whore." She further told Smith that "she would call her nothing but whore and harlot until she had been whipped and was married."

Parsing her language carefully, Brewster "denied the word whore" and said "she called her only harlot." The court rebuked her for such "railing language," saying, "Michael the Archangel durst not carry it so with the Devil, though he had matter enough against him."

Twelfth, Brewster had asked the Widow Potter why she was not received into the church again. Potter answered that it was "because she could not leave Edward Parker, yet if they could show her a rule for it, she would." Brewster then added that "Parker is not under scandal, yet because he gave not satisfaction to the elder, they will not let them marry."

Brewster acknowledged "the substance of this charge." Although the charge was seemingly innocuous to our modern ears, it piqued the interest of the court. An entirely new area of inquiry suddenly developed.

Parker and the Widow Potter were promptly brought before the court and asked about the matter. Potter admitted her conversation with Brewster, although she seemed to blame her loose tongue partly on the "cup of sack" (wine) Brewster had given her. But the real interest of the court was not in the substance of the conversation between Potter and Brewster but in the fact that this conversation had occurred at all. Potter, it turned out, was "an excommunicate person." The court explained to Brewster that "for her to eat, drink, and show such respect to excommunicate persons did expressly cross the rule."

Brewster and Potter began to argue as to who had drunk what. The argument could not have been helpful to Brewster's cause. Brewster denied that she had drunk with Potter. Potter responded that not only had they drunk together but also Brewster had drunk to her. Brewster replied that she "drank not, though she put the cup to her mouth," to which Potter opined that "from her carriage and outward appearance she apprehended she drunk, but could not say what quantity went down."

Brewster's remarks "gave much offense to the Court," but she kept on talking anyway. (This is usually a mistake for any party to a judicial proceeding.) She disclosed that she had counseled Potter and Parker to go before the magistrates to be married, but if the magistrates refused, "then before witnesses to take one another and go together." Brewster stated that she had said this in jest, but the court was not amused. In its view, the court told her, "notwithstanding any laughing or smiling countenance, the advice was seriously given."

At this point the court lodged yet another charge, a thirteenth, against Brewster. Contrary to an order given by the court, "she had retailed wine both out of doors by forbidden small parcels and had suffered workmen and others to sit drinking wine by pints and quarts within her house." Brewster responded that "it was when there was no other wine in town" and her customers "were either sick or had need of it." She added that three members of the court had themselves "sent to her for small parcels" and "hoped they would not lay snares for her." One of these imbibing members was Magistrate Richard Malbon. Malbon, we are told, "informed the court that Mrs. Brewster had said she would prove him a liar, which he hoped she could not do." In response to this, Parker offered to swear that Brewster had spoken these words "in a whisping way" and opined that, by that act alone, she had committed "an offensive, sinful miscarriage." The court chose not to have Parker swear to his statement.

Brewster was then asked if she had anything further to say. Indeed she had. We are told that "she was full of speech." This was something the court didn't like. "She was told that meekness and modesty would better become her in such a place." Duly reproved, "she fell to justify herself that she approved Mr. Davenport's ministry." But she also "laded the witnesses with reproach. All of them were liars." Elizabeth Smith was a "harlot," to boot.

Having heard the witnesses, the court made a procedural ruling. Brewster "had proved nothing to disable any of the witnesses." The witnesses "were therefore to give in evidence, severally upon oath, that the cause might come to a due issue." Accordingly, Smith, Hall, Parker, and the Widow Potter were placed under oath and "testified all the particulars they had respectively charged."

The court's attention then turned to Mrs. Moore. The principle witness against Moore was Job Hall, who we will recall had been chosen as a second eavesdropper by Elizabeth Smith because of his supposedly excellent memory. Hall, proving either his memory or his inventiveness, recounted to the court a lengthy prayer that Moore had given to the family of her daughter, Mrs. Leach. In her prayer, Moore had opined that the pastors and teachers given by Christ "had gone through the world and are now ascended into heaven. . . . Now, pastors and teachers are but the invention of men." This prayer opposed, "as he conceived," Reverend Davenport's sermon on Ephesians 4:11.[7] Additionally, "in conference with Mrs. Brewster," Moore had said that "a veil is before the eyes of ministers and people in this place, and until that be taken away, they cannot be turned to the Lord." Smith added that she "remembered the substance of what Job said and affirmed, but not all the particulars."

Moore denied the charge.

Thomas Kimberly continued the attack by recounting a lengthy scriptural argument he had had with Moore. Kimberly, citing Ephesians 4:11, had opined that "pastors and teachers are appointed for the work of the ministry," but Moore had responded that this passage referred to apostles now dead, and Kimberly "depended on the interpretation of men." She had, moreover, "answered in a great rage [that] she would go to none of them all for any truth of her salvation."

Moore acknowledged to the court that "Christ was present with the apostles in their travails to the end of the world, but for any other meanings she depended not on men's interpretations."

Governor Eaton then weighed in, telling Moore that "she was full of error notwithstanding the scriptures." In the governor's view, Christ's promise was "of a larger extent, that he would be with [the apostles] and their successors, such as in all ages and places he should employ." He further told Moore that "had she kept her error to herself, herself only had been hurt, but it is not to be suffered that she should blaspheme and revile the holy ordinances of Christ and the church and the people of God by spreading her errors [to] corrupt others and disturb the peace of the place."

Moore was then told that "the evidence was full and particular and sufficient to convict her, yet since she seemed not satisfied, the court would require oath." As in Brewster's case, the witnesses against Moore were then sworn and "upon oath testified what they had severally affirmed."

The court's attention finally turned to Mrs. Leach. Leach, the daughter of Mrs. Moore, was charged that, when asked if she would join the church, she told Brewster, "She sometime had a mind to join, but now declined it because she found so many untruths among them."

When asked for her response by the governor, Leach "readily owned it, confessing that she had said so." We are told that she "spoke uncomely for her sex and age. . . . Her carriage offended the whole court."

Given Leach's admission, the cases against the three women dissidents were completed. The cases, we are told, "were all ready for censure, but upon consideration of the nature and weight of the offenses, the magistrates and deputies conceived they were all proper for a higher court. By order therefore sentence was respited and referred to the court of magistrates for the jurisdiction."

With this referral to another court, the record closes. As to the fate of the three women dissidents, the record is silent.

❊❊❊❊❊

There is something in this case to offend virtually every modern sensibility. From a legal point of view, the exact charges against the three women dissidents were never made clear. Many of the alleged *facts* are reasonably clear by the end of the trial, although the eavesdropping servants had some trouble in keeping their stories straight. But exactly what rule of criminal or biblical law or mandate of New Haven Colony deportment had the three women broken? The formal charge seems to have been that they committed "several miscarriages of a public nature," which tells us virtually nothing.

The real charge seems to be that the women disagreed with the minister of the church on a variety of theological issues. The court made it clear that its function was to support the minister and that no dissent from the minister's word would be tolerated. In doing so, the court acted as an arm of the church and not as a neutral tribunal.

This does not mean that the court was lawless or entirely unfair in its procedure. The court continued the New Haven Colony tradition of recognizing the Bible as the source of the governing substantive law. Procedurally, the court found facts based on the testimony of witnesses, much of it ultimately sworn, and allowed each defendant to respond to each charge on an individual basis.

These procedural aspects are not, however, the most striking part of the trial to the modern eye. What stands out to us is the repressive nature of the whole enterprise. Issues of gender and class obviously loom large. The three defendants were women. It is certainly fair to ask whether such a proceeding would even have been brought against a man—especially a man of social importance—who had done the same thing. We are explicitly told that Leach's responses were "uncomely for her sex and age."

More than anything else, however, this proceeding was a heavy-handed exercise in thought control. The colony maintained the church. Theological disagreement with the church was not tolerated. Modern notions of freedom of thought and the dignity of the individual had no place in this society.

There was, in any event, little privacy to be found in the colony, either in theory or practice. No private conversation was safe. Not even private prayers were sacrosanct. Eavesdropping servants (and perhaps other eavesdroppers as well) were everywhere, and once a servant's employment had ended, there was nothing to stop him or her from going to the authorities. A colonist who said *anything*—not just in public speech but even in private prayer—that might give offense to persons in a position of power could be in real trouble. Under these circumstances, opportunities for blackmail must have abounded.

8

꧁꧂

THE

SHIPWRECK

꧁꧂

The General Court, which had not acted with conspicuous judiciousness in the Case of the Women Dissidents, demonstrated more impressive legal instincts when presented with a case claiming monetary damages arising out of the loss of a commercial boat.[1]

In the seventeenth century, as in modern times, admiralty law (as we call this area of the law) was a refined legal specialty. In England, cases of this description would have been heard in the High Court of Admiralty, which would have adjudicated those cases according to an elaborate body of customary maritime law built up over the centuries. The New Haven court, in contrast, had no such jurisprudential resources and necessarily was guided by its instincts. The result it reached, however, was consistent with the rule of law.

On January 5, 1647, John Evance appeared before the court claiming he had appointed John Charles as master of a shallop.[2] The shallop was to sail from New Haven to Guilford and Saybrook and back again to New Haven, carrying a cargo of peas and Madeira wine. Unhappily, the boat was broken up during the voyage, and the cargo was lost. When Evance first heard of this loss, "he apprehended it as an afflicting providence of God," but he later concluded that the loss had occurred because of Charles's negligence. Evance claimed that his damages, including the cargo and the boat itself, amounted to one hundred pounds. He wanted Charles to pay up.

The court was not Evance's first choice of a tribunal to hear his case. Initially, Evance and Charles had agreed to refer the matter to four arbitrators selected by themselves. The arbitrators, we are told, were "men that have long bred the sea and are well experienced in such cases." The parties bound themselves to "stand to" any arbitration award up to one hundred pounds. But the arbitrators couldn't agree on a decision. (This is a perennial hazard of any tribunal composed of an even number of decision makers.)

The arbitration agreement between Evance and Charles had provided for such a contingency. The arbitrators, being divided, jointly chose a fifth person to be the "umpire" in the case. The umpire chosen was a mariner named Robert Martin. Martin gave the parties "full hearing with their allegations and proofs" and gave judgment "in writing under his hand." His judgment was that "the shallop, boat and goods were lost by negligence and ought to be made good to the owners." Charles refused to obey Martin's award. Evance was thus "constrained to crave the help and justice" of the General Court.

The court began by asking Charles why he didn't submit to the arbitration award he had promised to obey. Charles responded that Martin had found that he (Charles) wasn't even in charge of the vessel. He had simply gone voluntarily on the vessel to Guilford to conduct some personal business. Besides, in Charles view, the boat "was lost for want of due provisions." It only had one anchor and cable; once the cable broke, nothing could be done. The court found this answer unresponsive and pressed the question. Would Charles stand by the arbitration award, or did the court have to decide the case on its own?

For reasons we can only guess at (perhaps the court's last question was construed as a broad hint), "at length by mutual consent the arbitration was waived." Evance would have to prove his case in court.

Before Evance could commence his proof, another complication arose. Both the governor and the deputy governor—both members of the court—had an interest "in part of the wine lost." They "desired liberty to rise, that they might neither judge, speak, nor sit in court, while a cause wherein themselves were concerned was in hand." The remainder of the court allowed the officials to recuse themselves.

Evance proceeded to address the remaining members of the court. He had originally appointed Sergeant Thomas Jefferies as master of the shallop, but three shipbuilders in New Haven needed Jefferies to go to Massachusetts to procure the rigging for their ship. Evance told the shipbuilders that he couldn't spare Jefferies unless someone else was procured to go in his place. Evance mentioned that Charles, apparently employed by the shipbuilders, might be just the man for the job. The shipbuilders spoke to Charles, who, according to Evance, "took time to consider of it and at last yielded and went." As it happened, Jefferies was later free to go anyway, but by that time Charles had the job.

Numerous witnesses, including the three shipbuilders—Jasper Crayne, John Wackman, and Joshua Atwater—were then called to testify under oath. Crayne said that when he went to Charles with Evance's offer, "Charles gave them no direct answer, but said he would consider of it." Wackman and Atwater testified that Evance told them that he had spoken with Charles himself prior to releasing Jefferies from his obligation.

Jefferies testified that the morning the boat was to depart, he went down to the water intending to go on the voyage, but he found Charles in the boat. Prior to this encounter, Jefferies "understood himself to be master of the said vessel."

John Griffin, one of the boat's two seamen, testified that he and his fellow seaman, Ralph Loynes, went to Evance's house to ask who was going to be the master of the boat. Evance responded, "Take you no care. John Charles or Sergeant Jefferies shall go along with you." Charles helped to stow the salt and, on the voyage itself, "accounted himself as master." Griffin and Loynes did what Charles commanded them to do.

Charles testified that "he went in the said boat as a freeman [a passenger rather than an employee], taking no charge upon him, and that the said John Evance made no agreement with him for voyages."

Evance responded that he had employed Charles for two years, during which Charles had "made several voyages as master." They had agreed upon wages the first time, and since then Charles had been content with the arrangement. Charles had never said he was going in the boat this time without wages, which was not surprising since Charles made his living by being a seaman.

Charles told the court that the former voyages were in vessels in which he had a one-quarter financial interest. The court pointed out to him, however, that he was still receiving wages and that "he was a man well known not to be so free of his sea labor as to go forth on a voyage as a freeman without wages in a vessel wherein himself was chief seaman and no one else fit to make charge." To this, Charles "made no reply, but affirmed no seaman could prove him master by the evidence given."

The court then turned to two other persons present in court and asked them "to express what they apprehended in the case." The two persons called upon were Tobias Dimock and Robert Martin, both of them "mariners, now or lately masters of ships."

Dimock testified that he had talked about the voyage with Ralph Loynes, one of the two seamen on the boat, who was now absent. Loynes told him that, after loading the boat with wine at Saybrook, a storm came up. The crew anchored the boat as far from shore as they could, but this wasn't far enough. The boat was still only "a quoit's cast from the shore," and they could not get her further off. Both Charles and the two seamen left the boat, and the vessel afterward drove onto the shore.

The court wanted more than this factual narrative. It asked Dimock "to declare his opinion, whether one shipped in the room or stead of a master of a vessel be not really the master of the said vessel and so to be accounted." Dimock answered that "if anyone were shipped in the room of a master of a ship and had his power, then he conceived he was master." Martin, the second mariner present in court, agreed with this opinion.

The court now told Evance that it wished him "to proceed and make proof that the boat and goods were cast away and lost through negligence." In response, John Griffin, one of the boat's seamen, was called and sworn.

Griffin testified that he had received instructions from Evance through Ralph Loynes, possibly (although he did not know) because Charles could not read. The boat had delivered some of its salt to Guilford and taken in peas. When the boat arrived in Saybrook, it delivered the rest of its salt and took in seven pipes of wine. They were caught in the storm before returning to New Haven. Helped by some local "Dutchmen," they anchored the boat as far from shore as they could and then came ashore. They left the boat because they were wet. The Dutchmen told them, "What will you do starving here. It were better for you to go on shore."

At this point, the governor reappears in the narrative. We will recall that the governor had recused himself from the case because he had an interest in the wine that had been lost in the wreck. But, at Charles's suggestion, the governor informed the court that the Dutchmen had told him that the vessel might have been saved if it had had another anchor and cable. The governor had told Evance about this so that he could hear the Dutchmen under oath, "but they came no more."

Lieutenant Joseph Godfrey testified that he had overheard the Dutchmen tell Evance that Charles's "neglect lay in letting the boat lie so long laden ashore, until the storm was so great that they could not carry her off so far as she should have been for her preservation."

Sergeant Jefferies testified that, in the area in question, seamen would drop their anchors "in the channel, for it is a dangerous place to ride at the wharf. . . . If the vessel had lain 20 or 30 fathoms farther from the shore, though the cable had broke, as the wind in the storm was, they might have gone clear of the point up the river, and as she lay, had the seamen been aboard, much might have been done for the boat's safety."

The court now turned to Charles. Must he "not conclude there was a great neglect in him?" Charles responded that "if he were master, he must confess there was a great neglect." He still pleaded, however, that "if the vessel had been provided with two cables and anchors, they would have held her."

The parties having nothing further to say on the question of negligence, the court turned to the issue of damages. It found, "by due proof," that five pipes of Madeira wine were wholly lost, at a cost of ten pounds a pipe. Almost fifty bushels of peas had been lost, at a cost of seven pounds. The cost of the boat, anchor, and cable came to ten pounds more.

"The premises being duly considered," the court made its findings.

First, given the evidence, Charles's testimony that he went on the boat as a freeman was "itself unreasonable and without any proof at all." Charles was, instead, the master of the boat.

Charles had not "exercised the ordinary care of a man taking charge for preservation of the vessel and goods." This conclusion was based on several grounds. First, "he did not, as reason requires and as the practice is of seamen in such cases, to let fall an anchor at a reasonable distance in the channel." Second, he had caused the vessel to wait too long at the wharf and "carried out no anchor to secure her." Third, after the storm began, "himself and the other seamen did all forsake her, whereas probably had they been in the vessel, they might have used other means to have saved her or some part of the goods now lost." Finally, Charles had "in court confessed that if he were proved master, there was a great neglect."

The court asked Charles if any of the damages were attributable to the neglect of the other seamen. When he made no such claim, the court, "for his gross negligence and unworthy carriage in such a place of trust," ordered him to pay Evance damages in the amount of sixty-seven pounds, "besides the ordinary court charges."

Evance moved the court "that he might have an execution granted, because John Charles is shortly to go to Virginia and thence to England." The court was hesitant "to grant execution so suddenly." Charles, however, told Evance that "he had 36 or 38 pounds in his own hands already towards it, and he would take order with Mr. Gilbert to pay the rest." Evance pronounced himself satisfied with this arrangement.

The "satisfaction" between the parties did not last long. A month later, Evance and Charles were back in court. Evance claimed that Charles had spent the intervening period of time slandering his good name.

Charles didn't help himself by initially ignoring a summons to appear in court. When Thomas Wheeler tracked him down to order him to return to New Haven, Charles responded that for Evance "to take away his money and so deal with him was the Judasest trick that either he or ever man was served." Wheeler, assisted by a Native American, overcame Charles's resistance and returned him to New Haven on board a ship. Charles told Wheeler that he "had been wronged by Mr. Evance, however now he must lie at the mercy of the court." Although Charles added that he "intended no contempt of the court," another witness quoted him as saying that "they had got sixty pounds from him, but if any wise man were in the plantation, it had not been so."

As might be expected, the court was not amused. "For his contemptuous carriages and vile expressions, tending to the defaming the Court for doing justice according to their light," Charles was ordered to "pay twenty pounds to the jurisdiction."

The court then turned to the charge of slander. Evance told the court that "Charles had gone up and down in a slanderous way reproaching him and saying he had cheated him and said he was as unmerciful as a dog."

Another witness, John Mose, stated that Charles had said that Evance "had broken his promise once or twice in money or beaver lent him." Charles acknowledged saying this but claimed Evance in fact owed him wages. Evance responded that Charles had asked him to defer payment of some wages while Charles went to England to settle some accounts and that he fully intended to deal with Charles faithfully.

Lieutenant Robert Seely told the court that Charles had said, "There was no more mercy in Mr. Evance than a dog, and when he had any advantage he would use it."

The court had heard enough. For defaming Evance and "wounding him in his credit and faithfulness, which is to undo him so far as lay in his power," it ordered Charles to pay Evance fifty pounds.

At the close of the proceeding, "Charles acknowledged the ground of all these words was the boat."

⚬⚬⚬⚬⚬

"The ground of all these words was the boat." Charles's parting words in the Shipwreck Case raise an issue debated among judges in every era. If litigants in a hotly contested case receive a fair trial, will the losing party in that case accept the judgment? It is quite evident that Charles did not accept the judgment that he was responsible for the loss of the boat.

Judges like to tell themselves that what litigants want more than anything else is the opportunity to be heard. If a litigant's claims are fully heard by a fair and unbiased tribunal, the theory goes, the fairness of the judicial process itself will provide a source of satisfaction for the litigants, even for the losing party. This is a beguiling theory but, of course, one not always true in practice. Some losing parties will inevitably be sore losers. Charles was certainly one of them. And while it is impossible to be sure across the centuries whether Charles really was the master of the boat in question and whether his negligence, if any, was really the cause of the boat's loss, the way the shipwreck claim was handled by the New Haven court looks surprisingly fair to the modern eye.

From a modern legal point of view, the party who really had a right to complain about the way that the court handled the shipwreck claim was not Charles but Evance. Remember that Evance and Charles had originally agreed to submit their claim to arbitration. Martin, the umpire chosen according to the arbitration agreement, had decided in Evance's favor. Had Evance and Charles come into a modern court in the wake of completed arbitration, the case would have been a short one. Arbitration agreements are ruthlessly enforced in the modern judicial world.

But Evance (perhaps under some pressure from the court) agreed to waive the arbitration and take on the obligation of proving his case in court. Adjudicating in an area not governed by biblical precepts, the court went to great lengths to scrupulously find the facts. While the court heard numerous witnesses presented by the parties, it was particularly impressive in its use of outside experts.

The members of the General Court may well have had limited personal experience with admiralty issues, and witnesses called by a party can always have an axe to grind. The court, finding two persons present with actual experience as masters of ships, called upon those persons to supply it with relevant information. The court was not so interested in narrative information concerning what had happened to the boat in question, the type of information that ideally comes from eyewitnesses to the event, as in what we would now call "expert opinion" evidence. It specifically wanted to know the customary law of the maritime community.

Is someone, the court asked, "shipped in the room or stead of a master of a vessel not really the master of the said vessel and so to be accounted"? By asking questions like this of persons much more likely to know the answer than members of the court itself, the court was endeavoring to reach a decision consistent with customary maritime law. For this effort, the court deserves much credit.

9

≈≈≈≈

THE

FAULTY

SHOES

≈≈≈≈

In December 1647, the General Court was called upon to decide another case arising from the problems of local commerce, this one dealing with faulty shoes.[1] As it had earlier in the same year in the Shipwreck Case, the court made imaginative use of outside experts to arrive at its decision.

John Meges, a New Haven leather and shoe merchant, told the court that he had made a bargain with Henry Gregory, a Stratford shoemaker. Gregory was to make Meges fourteen dozen shoes, for which Meges would pay him twelve pence a pair. Meges paid forty-eight shillings of this amount up front and was to pay an additional six pounds when Gregory had done half the work. The work was to be done "well and sufficiently." Gregory made thirteen dozen of the shoes, "but they are all naught and fall to pieces, some in a week, some in 14 days' time." This, Meges said, caused him much reputational damage far and wide. "At Connecticut, Totoket, Guilford, Stratford, Fairfield, they all cry out, and some think the plaintiff worthy to be put in prison." Meges had also lost a contract to supply thirty pounds' worth of shoes to John Evance (whom we remember from the Shipwreck Case). Evance had turned back the offered shoes as "unmerchantable." In fact, Meges said, "many people have shunned to buy any ware of him."

Meges described the problem with Gregory's shoes. Gregory, he said, "has not only made the ware badly but has spoiled the leather by laying [the shoes] in the sand." As a result, some of the shoes were rotten, and all of them were covered with sand and had to be washed to be made clean. Moreover, the shoes were not made according to specification. Gregory should have made some with wooden heels but failed to do so. Some shoes were a size too short, and some that were size 9 were marked with a 10. Gregory asked for a last. Meges sent him one, but the mistakes continued as before.

Gregory had a different story to tell. Meges's description of the bargain between the parties was incomplete. Meges had initially sold Gregory a hide for the price of forty-eight shillings. Out of this hide, Gregory was to make four dozen shoes, for which Meges was to pay him the same sum—forty-eight shillings.[2] Gregory completed part of this bargain "before the other bargain." Meges "saw the ware and accepted it." Meges agreed to take the rest of the shoes, but Gregory told him that "he would make no more of such leather."

Meges promised to supply Gregory with better leather and to procure hemp from the Connecticut Colony to sew the shoes. He didn't follow up on this, so Gregory "was forced to buy flax at 18 pence" and sew the shoes with flax. When Meges wanted more shoes, Gregory "minded him of his promise to bring better leather and told him, this is as bad or worse than the first, that if he had not better leather he would do no more." Gregory added,

"It is pity, but the tanner should be hanged which tanned it, for he cozens the country."

Gregory didn't place all the blame on the tanner. In his opinion, Meges bore much of the fault in the matter. Meges had supplied him with hide regardless of whether it was tanned enough or not. Gregory wanted to sew the shoes with hemp, but Meges said that "the thread would last as long as the leather." Based on this representation, Gregory "went on and did all the work, all but one dozen, but he neglected to fetch them away." Gregory took out the best pair of shoes he could find among the first four dozen he had made and gave them to Adam Blackman's son. "In a short time, they tore out in the whole leather." This was because the leather was "so bad." As for the size markings on the shoes, Gregory simply followed Meges's instructions. According to Gregory, he "lost 15 weeks' time by the negligence of John Meges."

Gregory finally told the court that he had made "the wooden heels shoes otherwise than he appointed," because he had "taken those rands to make welts for the plain shoes."[3] "For this, the court blamed him, telling him he should have foreborn making them 'til he had been supplied with materials." Meges added that he "sent welts with all the shoes he sent."

The parties having spoken, "witnesses were called and examined." These witnesses did not appear in person. Rather, it appears, they had made pretrial statements under oath, several of them before the governor. The sworn statements were then admitted into evidence.

Jonathan Sargant testified that he had purchased from Meges a pair of russet shoes, closed in the inside at the side seams. He wore them two or three times to a neighbor's house and twice to a meeting about forty "rods" away (a rod is five meters). The night after the second meeting, he walked down to the water, about sixty rods away. When he came back, the sole of one shoe had fallen off and the other one was about to do so. He got the soles sewn back on and wore the shoes occasionally for a week or two. "Then the insoles and outsoles and all fell from the upper leather." He never wore the shoes again.

Thomas Whiteway testified that he bought from Meges a pair of russet shoes closed in the inside at the side seams. He wore them three or four days and then the outsoles ripped. He sewed them again, wore them three or four days more, and the insoles and the welts came off. He sewed them a third time, and the upper leather, seams, heels, and sides ripped. Whiteway thought that "Meges should be put in prison for so cozening the country."

John Parmele of Guilford testified that he bought a similar pair of shoes from Meges. They lasted six or seven days before they ripped.

Samuel Nettleton of Totoket testified that he had bought a similar pair of shoes from Meges for his wife. She put them on on the Lord's Day, and three days later they were ripped. The soles of the shoes, however, were "good, neither shrunk nor horny that I could perceive."

Mark Meges testified that he had gone to Stratford to fetch the shoes made by Gregory for John Meges. Mark Meges "found the shoes lying in the sand, many of them being partly covered with the sand, both within and without, so that he was forced to take away the sand with his hands to come at them." Gregory "washed them in water to wash away the sand and filth from them." Mark Meges had seen "the old man work with a very great awl and a small thread, with very little wax" and "blamed him for it."

The records state that "other testimonies were delivered in writing to the Court to the same purpose, but not upon oath."

Gregory responded, "It was the badness of the leather which

was the cause of the shoes ripping and falling apieces, for the leather was horny and not tanned." The court told him to "prove that."

John Evance told the court that he had talked with Adam Blackman about the shoes. Blackman said that "after two or three days' wearing, the leather was like flaps of a shoulder of mutton." Evance had tried to sell some of these shoes to someone else, but "the leather was so bad that the party would not have them."

Blackman told the court that his son had a pair of these shoes, which lasted about three weeks before they "broke in the whole leather." He used some of the leather to mend another pair of shoes for another son, but within days the leather "being wet, was spoiled."

Gregory's son, Juda Gregory, testified under oath that he had seen some of the leather that Meges had supplied to his father, and "some of it was so horny that, according to his judgment, no man could make shoes to pass his word on them to hold. Also, shoes so tainted, though they might seem to be tanned, yet they would not hold that a man was able to justify himself or the leather in it." The leather was bad "because it was horny and so little that it would not come together." As for the shoes lying in the sand, the shoes that he had seen had lain "without any damage, without any sand in any pair that he could discern." He wasn't sure, however, that he had seen the same shoes described by Mark Meges.

Moses Wheeler testified under oath that Meges had left some leather at his house for Gregory. "The next day, his wife took up some of it in her hand and said she thought it was tainted and, pulling it between her hands, it did tear with ease." On another occasion, he heard Gregory say that he was "sick of that leather and that he should never have credit of it for his work."

Gregory's daughter, described by the records as "the wife of William Crooker," testified that "when Goodman Meges came for the shoes, he saw them lie on a sandy bench in the cellar, and he said he liked the lying of them very well, saying to her father he could not lay them better." When her father found "fault with the horniness of the leather, that the flax would not hold it," Meges told him that "the next week he would go to Connecticut and get him hemp, but he said he thought the flax would last as long as that leather." When her father "blamed the tanner for the leather not being well tanned, Goodman Meges answered he could not blame the tanner so much, for he was fain to take it out before it was tanned." She said "she saw it tear in pieces when her father put it on the last."

The court, having heard this evidence, "did think there was a fault in both, and that the country was much wronged in this way." Given this opinion, it decided that expert evidence was called for. Specifically, it was "willing to call in some workmen, both shoemakers and tanners, that they might see it and judge whose the fault was and so give into the court what light they could."

The court had some shoes brought from Evance, "which were some of the best of them," and called three shoemakers and two tanners "to take those shoes aside and view them well, and if there be cause, rip some of them, that they may give into the court according to their best light, the cause of the damage." The experts did so, and one of them, Lieutenant Robert Seely, a shoemaker, spoke "in the name of the rest." Seely reported as follows: "The leather is very bad, not tanned nor fit to be sold for serviceable leather, but it wrongs the country, nor can a man make good work of a great deal of it. And we find the workmanship bad also. First there is not sufficient stuff put in the thread, and instead of hemp it is flax, and the stitches are too long, and the threads not drawn home, and there wants wax on the thread. The awl is too big for the thread. We ordinarily put in 7 threads, and here is but 5. So that according to our best light, we lay the cause both upon the workmanship and the badness of the leather."

Hearing this testimony, Gregory "seemed to be convinced that he had not done his part but then laid the fault on Goodman Meges, that he was the more slight in it through his encouragement, who said to him, 'Flap them up. They are to go far enough.'"

More witnesses now came forward and testified under oath. William Hooke Jr. testified that he clearly remembered Gregory making shoes in his shop. Meges came in and said to Gregory, "Flap them up together. They are to go far enough." John Gregory testified that he had heard the same statement.

Goodwife Meges testified that her husband told Gregory "at the fair in September" that he was "discouraged to send him any more work because his work was naught, though he had more work ready cut out."

Gregory's son, John Gregory, testified, "About the time of the bargain he gave Goodman Meges some cautions, because his father was old, and his eyesight failed him, and he durst not employ him himself, for he could not do as he had done."

Evance testified that "the main reason" he had rejected the shoes offered by Meges "was the badness of the leather, though he also excepted against the workmanship."

The court called upon Meges "to propound his damage." In response, Meges itemized five items of damages: "First in his name, secondly damages to Mr. Evance, thirdly his ware being turned upon his hand, fourthly hindrance in his trade, [and] fifthly money paid several men for satisfaction."

The parties having no more to say, the court "considering the case as it had been presented, debated and proved, found them both faulty." It delivered the following judgment:

Goodman Gregory had transgressed rules of righteousness, both in reference to the country and to Goodman Meges, though his fault to Goodman Meges is more excusable because of that encouragement Goodman Meges gave him to be slight in his workmanship, though he should not have taken any encouragement to do evil, [and] should have complained to some magistrate and not have wrought such leather in such a manner into shoes, by which the country, or whosoever wears them, must be deceived. But the greater fault and guilt lies upon John Meges for putting such untanned, horny, unserviceable leather into shoes and for encouraging Goodman Gregory to slight workmanship upon a motive that the shoes were to go far enough, as if rules of righteousness reached not other places and countries.

The court proceeded to sentence and ordered Goodman Meges "to pay 10 pounds as a fine to the jurisdiction, with satisfaction to every particular person as damage shall be required and proved." The court further ordered that "none of the faulty shoes be carried out of the jurisdiction to deceive men, the shoes deserving to be burnt than sold if there had been a law to that purpose; yet in the jurisdiction they may be sold, but then only as deceitful ware, and the buyer may know them to be such." It also ordered Goodman Gregory, "for his slight, faulty workmanship and fellowship in the deceit, to pay 5 pounds as a fine to the jurisdiction and to pay the charges of the Court, and that he require nothing of Goodman Meges for his loss of time in this work, whether it were more or less." The members of the court thought "themselves speedily called and seriously to consider how these deceits may be, for time to come, prevented or duly punished."

This was not the last the court was to hear of John Meges. In June 1648, Meges was again before the court for a pair of shoes made of unsealed leather sold to Moses Wheeler. Questioned by the court, Meges "pretended ignorance that leather in men's houses should be sealed." He acknowledged that he had a piece of leather in his house, "though he know it was both unsealed and horny, not tanned," and had made Wheeler "a small pair of shoes from that leather."

Remembering the case that Meges had brought against Gregory the previous December and what then appeared to be Meges's "inward conviction and suitable sorrow," the court was "deeply offended at this passage." It did not know how many shoes of faulty, unsealed leather Meges had made and sold in the intervening time, "but in this one pair, several evils appear." First, Meges had shown "contempt of authority in breaking an order wherein himself with others had been advised with and had approved it." Second, he had shown "continued unrighteousness in selling a small pair of shoes made [with] both upper leathers and soles of faulty leather at so high a price, not acquainting the buyer with any defect or purpose of any restitution if the shoes proved bad." Third, there was "much appearance of guile in his late repentance, returning so soon to the same sin for which he had voluntarily and publicly judged himself." Given these aggravating circumstances, the court ordered Meges "to pay twenty shillings to the Town as a fine, beside due satisfaction to Moses Wheeler when it shall be required."

Although the subject matter of the Case of the Faulty Shoes was humble enough, the case shows the General Court as a surprisingly creative judicial institution. Not all of this creativity would be applauded today. By some alchemy, a civil case for damages was transformed in the twinkling of an eye, and without apparent warning to the litigants, into a criminal case. Two men who had come to court to resolve a contract dispute suddenly found themselves hit with heavy fines payable to the jurisdiction. The modern due process requirement that parties to a proceeding receive fair notice of what is at stake was not observed.

In other ways, however, the court was remarkably prescient. Two positive attributes of the proceeding stand out. First, the court correctly looked beyond the outward form of the proceeding—an action for damages between two men based on a commercial shoe contract—to see that this was a case that affected the *public*. Regardless of who was at fault here—whether the shoes sold by Meges were bad because of faulty workmanship by Gregory or faulty leather supplied by Meges—the end result was that members of the public were paying good money for bad shoes. Quite apart from the question of whether Meges had lost money because of Gregory or Gregory had lost money because of Meges, the real victims here were people like Jonathan Sargant and Thomas Whiteway who were wearing shoes that fell apart after a few days. From the public's point of view, this was an intolerable situation. In a famous phrase adopted by the Supreme Court in a regulatory case two centuries later, the shoe trade was "affected with a public interest."[4] In a case of this description, the court was right to perceive that it had an important role to play in protecting the public.

Second, in procedural terms, the court was particularly impressive in appointing a panel of experts, drawn from two different disciplines, to help it obtain the technical expertise necessary to decide the case. Looking back through the lens of history, the court's use of outside experts prefigured a landmark judicial use of independent expertise in the twentieth century—also, by coincidence, involving the shoe industry.

In the late 1940s, Charles E. Wyzanski Jr., a federal district judge in Boston, was assigned an enormous antitrust case involving the shoe industry. After two years of pretrial proceedings, he found that, to correctly decide the case, he needed the assistance of an economist. Wyzanski had close ties to Harvard University, and a friend in the Economics Department recommended Carl Kaysen, then a new assistant professor with research interests in antitrust issues. In an unprecedented move, Wyzanski appointed Kaysen—whose instruction in legal matters was mostly informal—as his law clerk. Kaysen worked with the judge on the case for two years. The shoe industry's challenge to his appointment was unavailing. "In rejecting the challenge, Judge Wyzanski said in court that he was not obliged to notify counsel when he read books on economics. Why then could counsel properly object to his talking privately to an economist in the role of law clerk in pursuit of the same kind of information and analysis he might seek from books?"[5] Judge Wyzanski's antitrust decision was eventually affirmed on the merits by the Supreme Court.[6]

The humble Case of the Faulty Shoes presented similar jurisprudential issues. In a case simply involving two private parties, a forceful argument can be put forth that a court's decision should be made strictly on the evidence submitted by the parties. But in a case "affected with a public interest," the court has a greater responsibility. The *public* has an interest in seeing that the case is decided correctly. If a correct decision requires technical expertise, the court must find some way of obtaining that expertise. In finding the expertise necessary to decide the Case of the Faulty Shoes, the General Court displayed a boldness and imagination that a modern court might envy.

10

·ᏳᏳᏕᏔ·

THE

DRUNKEN

SAILORS

·ᏳᏳᏔᏔ·

On August 1, 1648, the General Court heard the Case of the Drunken Sailors.[1] In the midst of hearing the vivid details of an epic brawl, the court was confronted with a classic case of statutory interpretation.

Eight men appeared before the court: Robert Bassett, a New Haven planter; William Badger and Charles Higenson, crewmen of the ship *Susan*; and Thomas Toby "and four others who came lately from Boston to work upon the ship here built."[2] The court was informed that the previous Saturday night, the defendants had committed "several miscarriages, to the great provocation of God, the disturbance of the peace, and to such a height of disorder that strangers wondered at it, and Robert Bassett himself confessed he had not seen the like since he came."

The records' description of the brawl is especially vivid. After their work was finished on Saturday night, some of the *Susan*'s company came on shore and "met with the master and owner of a pinnace lately come in from Boston and four of the workmen for the ship built here." A total of ten men went to Bassett's house and "called for sack." Citing the local liquor law (more of this in a moment), Bassett told his patrons he "might not draw less than three quarts." That was fine with the merry company, and after Bassett had drawn three quarts, he ended up drawing them an additional three quarts for good measure. Unsurprisingly, "some of the company drank to excess and distemper."

This led to trouble. The owner of the pinnace, in his cups, called the boatswain of the *Susan* "Brother Loggerhead." The boatswain took exception to this appellation, and the two of them went out of the house. Now the battle began in earnest:

> The master of the pinnace and the boatswain . . . fall first to wrestling, then to blows, and therein grew to that fierceness that the master of the pinnace thought the boatswain would have pulled out his eyes, and the marks of the blows appeared some days after upon his face; and in this rage and distemper they tumbled on the ground, down the hill into the creek and mire, shamefully wallowing therein; and had they not been parted, they might have proceeded to further mischief, for Charles Higenson, distempered as it seems with drink, in a way of siding with the boatswain, grew quarrelsome, wherein the owner of the pinnace, being affrighted, ran about the street crying, "Ho, the watch. Ho, the watch."

> The watch, being then in that part of the town walking the rounds, made haste and for the present stopped the course of the disorder, but in this rage and distemper, the boatswain fell a swearing . . . as if he were not only angry with men but would provoke the high and blessed God. After they were thus parted, the master of the pinnace went to the water side, but the season

not serving to go on board, he returned to Robert Bassett's house, and there the boatswain fell upon him again and thereby frightened Robert Bassett's wife and child. Robert Bassett moved therewith, thrust the owner of the pinnace out of doors and told him (as himself confesses) that, "If he had him in place . . . he would beat out his teeth," or, as Thomas Toby (Robert Bassett's witness) relates it, he "would make him suck as long as he lived."

The parties acknowledging "the particulars in substance," the court turned to the men before it. The court deemed Bassett to be the worst malefactor of the lot. It was particularly incensed by his self-serving interpretation of the New Haven Colony's liquor law. The law seemingly referred to was one promulgated by the New Haven court in 1645. That law decreed the following: "To prevent much sin and inconvenience which may grow by disorderly meetings and drinkings, it is ordered that none of or belonging to this Plantation shall either directly or indirectly within their houses, cellars, or other places, sell or deliver out any sort of wine or strong liquors by retail, namely by pottles,[3] quarts, pints or the like, without express license from this court, under such penalty and fine as the monthly court, upon due consideration of the miscarriage or contempt, shall see cause to impose."[4]

There was probably never a literal "three quart rule." Bassett merely thought he had figured a clever way around the court's decree. The court, however, found his view "a most perverse interpretation and abuse of an order, as if the court would further drunkenness, forcing men to drink more than they desired, whereas he should have drawn none at all in that way; the order being expressly made and penned to suppress such disorderly meetings and drinkings."

The court found Bassett "guilty of the breach of a known express order of the general court." He was ordered to pay five pounds as a fine to the town. The boatswain, whose subsequent good behavior had been vouched for by John Evance and Robert Martin, was fined forty shillings. Charles Higenson was fined ten shillings, and Thomas Toby, who had helped Bassett in drawing the wine, was fined five shillings. The four workers on the boat being built were guilty only of "being in company in this disorderly meeting" and were released with a "warning against all future disorder." The fate of the owner of the pinnace is unknown. It is unlikely that he lingered in the colony after hearing Bassett's threats.

⊰⊱⊰⊱

While the Case of the Drunken Sailors has obvious dramatic interest, its principal legal interest is the General Court's encounter with a classic problem of statutory interpretation. The law forbade persons from selling alcohol in "pottles, quarts, pints or the like." Bassett sold it in three-quart servings. Did he violate the law?

The question whether laws should be construed according to their letter or their purpose is as old as the legal system itself. No matter how carefully a law is drafted (and laws are not always drafted carefully), a situation will arise that the drafters of the law could not have anticipated. When this happens (and it happens surprisingly often), it is the duty of the court to ascertain the actual "purpose" of the law.

In 1869 the Supreme Court decided a famous case illustrating this problem. An old postal law provided that any person who "shall knowingly and willfully obstruct the passage of the mail, or of any carrier" commits a crime. A man named Farris was wanted for murder. Kirby, a sheriff, found Farris and arrested him. Unfortunately for Kirby, it turned out that Farris was a mail carrier, and a grand jury indicted him for breaking the postal law. Had Farris in fact broken the law? On review, the Supreme Court said no. It explained that "all laws should receive a sensible construction. General terms should be so limited in their application as not to lead to injustice, oppression, or an absurd consequence. It will always, therefore, be presumed that the legislature intended exceptions to its language which would avoid results of this character. The reason of the law in such cases should prevail over its letter."[5]

This was the judicial approach taken by the General Court in the Case of the Drunken Sailors. Its function was not to read the law literally, as Bassett had attempted to do, but to ascertain what it was that the promulgators of the law were attempting to accomplish. In this case, the judicial task was not attended with much difficulty. The purpose of the law in question was stated in the law itself. The law was expressly intended to prevent "disorderly meetings and drinkings." Serving alcohol to a group of sailors three quarts at a time was obviously likely to result in just such behavior. It is difficult to fault the court for its interpretation of the law.

11

〰〰〰

THE COMPETING
CLAIMANTS

〰〰〰

On July 3, 1649, John Evance (the shipowner we previously met in the Shipwreck Case) came to the General Court with a real stumper of a case.[1] Evance claimed that the defendant, William Westerhousen, owed him 255 pounds for money he (Evance) had expended on a ship, the *Swallow*, now owned by Westerhousen. Westerhousen responded that he owned the *Swallow* free and clear. Each party had a plausible claim. Somehow the court had to sort out the matter.

Evance told the court the following story. The *Swallow* was partly owned by a merchant named Daniel Peirse. (We don't know who the other owners were.) Peirse needed money to prepare the ship for a commercial voyage to Barbados. To finance the voyage, Evance lent Peirse a sum of money, and in return Peirse agreed to pay Evance 255 pounds "to be paid at Barbados in cotton wool."[2] This agreement was memorialized in a bill signed by Peirse; Steven Reekes, the master of the vessel; and witnesses Governor Theophilus Eaton and Reverend John Davenport. We don't have the actual text of the agreement, but Evance construed it as guaranteeing that he would "be paid the money by the ship, for the money was expended upon the ship, without which she was not fit to proceed upon any voyage." Although Evance characterized his case as "an action of debt for 255 pounds sterling," he made his actual demand in his argument. "He demandeth the vessel." He was no longer looking for a sum of money. He wanted the ship.

Westerhousen responded with the record of a court proceeding in Virginia and written testimony from a Virginia sheriff that he proceeded to read to the New Haven court. The Virginia documents are summarized rather than quoted in the New Haven records, but from the parties' remarks and the subsequent findings of the New Haven court, we can piece together what they say. The ship departed for Barbados, but "an afflicting providence" kept it "at sea and from her port at Barbados 'til mariners' wages have eaten out her value." Finally, after a futile voyage of thirteen months, the ship landed in Virginia, never having made it to Barbados. The sailors brought an action in a Virginia court for their wages, and after a trial the Virginia court granted them the ship. A Virginia sheriff then officially delivered the ship to the sailors. The sailors subsequently sold the ship to Westerhousen, and—in his opinion—he owned it fair and square. At least some of the sailors were in court to support his claim.

The Virginia record did not reflect that Evance had received any official notice of the proceedings in that colony. Notwithstanding this, the sailors testified that an attorney for Evance "was in court when the cause was cast."

Evance replied that the sailors were to be paid up front out of the money that he had lent Peirse. (It was apparently for this reason that Peirse had needed the money to finance the voyage in the first place.) In Evance's opinion, "the wages must be cleared when they departed." In any event, Evance calculated the crew's wages as amounting to about twenty pounds a month. For a thirteen-month voyage, he figured the crew must have come out about even. Moreover, "seeing that they knew that the ship was made over, they might have chosen whether they would have gone or no."

The General Court was thus presented with a problem that would perplex a court of any era. If two different persons present plausible claims to the same item of property, who should prevail? Each side made a forceful argument, and whichever side lost would be out of a great deal of money. How should the court resolve the case?

Governor Eaton's interest was piqued. (He did not recuse himself despite the fact that he had personally witnessed the original contract between Evance and Peirse.) As would a law professor of the present day, he asked the sailors present in the courtroom some hypothetical questions. Suppose, he said, that "a ship is upon a voyage and, putting in a port by the way, through some stress of weather, wants a new suit of sails or a cable and anchor. The mariners buy them and engage to make payment at her port of discharge, if there the ship shall come to be sold for men's wages, shall these sails pay them their wages, which they could not have earned without them?" Or suppose again, the governor continued, "a ship comes into a harbor [and] wants repair. A workman works upon the ship [and] earns 20 pounds, but before the ship goes away, there falls a difference, and men call for wages and the ship comes to be sold. Shall not the carpenter be paid for his work?"

The sailors responded to these questions with an answer well known to law students (and judges) of any era. "They could not say." Nevertheless, the sailors maintained, "the ship is theirs by order of the court of Virginia."

The parties had no more to say, and the court proceeded to its decision. It reasoned that "had the ship arrived in due season at Barbados, Mr. Evance might have required his debt from the owners, and the ship, with her furniture, was engaged for it." That, however, did not happen. The ship having put in at Virginia, "the mariners had (as the case stood) the first and chief right to their wages. . . . The tenor and import of Mr. Evance's deed is to secure his debt from the owners by the ship and her furniture, not from the mariners out of the wages which should grow due from hence to Barbados or any other port. [The court] saw not therefore how they could justly dispossess the mariners (or Mr. Westerhousen claiming from or under them) of the ship granted them by sentence of court in Virginia." Westerhousen kept the ship, and Evance left the courtroom empty handed.

⬥⬥⬥⬥⬥

Was the General Court right? The answer depends in part on whether you view the case as presenting a substantive or a procedural issue. The distinction between substance and procedure is one learned by first-year law students, but in a complicated case such as this, where each side is waving one of the opposing banners, it can still keep experienced judges up at night.

Evance looked at the case as presenting a *substantive* problem of law. He had a contract. The contract had been witnessed by none other than the governor of the colony and the minister of the church. The contract said he was entitled to 255 pounds. Evance had fully performed his part of the contract by lending the money to Peirse. Thus far, no one had paid him a penny. In his view, he was fully entitled to the money as a matter of substantive law.[3]

Westerhousen, in contrast, looked at the case as presenting a *procedural* problem. There had been a court proceeding in

Virginia. Although Evance hadn't been officially notified of the Virginia proceeding, he had an attorney representing him there anyway, so no harm, no foul. There was no other criticism of the Virginia proceeding. The Virginia court had awarded the ship to the sailors, fair and square. Westerhousen had subsequently purchased it from the sailors, fair and square. He therefore owned the boat, fair and square, regardless of the terms of some long-ago contract to which he wasn't even a party.

If this case were litigated in a modern American court, the answer to these competing claims would be easy. Article IV of the Constitution requires that "Full Faith and Credit shall be given in each State to the public Acts, records, and judicial Proceedings of every other State." Under what we call the Full Faith and Credit Clause, a judge in one state must fully honor a judicial decision made in another state, even if the judge in the second state thinks the judge in the first state was dead wrong. This is one of the ways the Constitution works to bind the nation together. In modern times, Westerhousen could simply present an official record from the Virginia court and the case would be over.

The Case of the Competing Claimants was, however, tried in 1649. The U.S. Constitution would not be a gleam in anyone's eye for well over a hundred years. Neither New Haven nor Virginia was bound by anything like the Full Faith and Credit Clause. In any event, New Haven and Virginia were not coequal states joined in a national union. They were fellow British colonies, but their legal status, for purposes of this case, was more akin to that of independent nations. Their courts were under no official obligation to credit the judgments of any other courts. The situation was a little like that of a modern American court presented with a judgment delivered by a court sitting in Paraguay or Zanzibar.

Unless a treaty or an American statute requires obedience to the foreign judgment,[4] no obedience is required.

But cases pertaining to ships involve special considerations. Because ships are mobile (that's why people use them) and routinely travel between different countries, courts have subjected them to special rules for centuries. At an early stage of its existence, the Supreme Court decided that, quite apart from the Full Faith and Credit Clause, when an action is brought against a ship[5] in a foreign court, the judgment of that court is conclusive with respect to the ship, even if a later judge in this country thinks that the first judgment was wrong. As Chief Justice John Marshall explained, "By such sentence, the right of the former owner is lost, and a complete title given to the person who claims under the decree."[6] This treatment allows international commerce to be conducted according to predictable rules known to everyone in advance.

The General Court knew nothing of this in 1649. There was no indication that it was even aware of the English admiralty rules of its own time. Nevertheless, it reached a sensible result that is difficult to criticize from a modern point of view. And the decision is notable for being perhaps the first decision of any American court to give credit to the decision of another American court. In that respect, the General Court was at the forefront of a legal tradition that would one day help to create a nation.

12

❀

THE FRISKY

COUPLE

❀

On the same day that it heard the Competing Claimants, the General Court heard charges of fornication against Thomas Meekes and Rebecka Turner.[1] Surprisingly, William Westerhousen, the winning party in the Competing Claimants, was to play an unsought role in this case as well.

Governor Theophilus Eaton had previously heard the Frisky Couple "in a private way." He thought the matter serious enough to be presented in court, and now the unhappy couple was called to appear in public "to answer to their sinful miscarriage in matter of fornication."

Meekes started the proceeding with a full confession. "He could say nothing against what hath been declared but it is true, and he desires to judge and condemn himself for it in the sight of God and his people." Turner also acknowledged that the things charged were true. Although she had originally said that "Meekes had had to do with her but once," she now admitted that "it was oftener."

Although this was enough to dispose of the case at hand, the governor—who had caused the couple to be presented in court in the first place—now decided to expand the scope of the inquiry.

He had, he declared to the court, "heard of sundry passages which render Mr. Westerhousen suspicious in this business." The governor proceeded to describe six charges against Westerhousen.

First, Turner had said "she could not love Mr. Goodanhousen, but she could love Mr. Westerhousen."[2] Westerhousen responded that "she said not so to him." Turner agreed "it was not to him but to somebody in the house."

Second, Turner reported that Westerhousen had told her that "if his wife was dead, he would make her his wife." Westerhousen denied that he had said this. Turner responded in court that "it is true that she said so, but [she] cannot tell but she might be mistaken."

Third, Westerhousen gave Turner "sundry gifts to a considerable value." This troubled her stepfather, Samuel Goodanhousen,[3] who told Westerhousen that "he could maintain his daughter without his gifts." Westerhousen said that this referred to an incident "at the fair," where Daniel Peirse (whom we remember as the original shipowner in the Case of the Competing Claimants) "gave her lace for a handkerchief" and Westerhousen gave her cloth.

Fourth, Westerhousen "carried her behind him to the farm." This was presumably on a horse. Westerhousen replied that, on the night in question, "she was going to the farm very late, [and] her mother pitied her. He bid them set her behind him, and he would carry her, and so he did."

Fifth, as he was coming from the farm, he told William Wooden and Henry Humerstone he had not been there, but when Wooden and Humerstone asked Turner about the matter, she said "he was there, and she knew not that he had been anywhere else." Westerhousen denied this, "whereupon their oaths were required." Wooden and Humerstone then confirmed their stories under oath.

Sixth, Wooden and Humerstone additionally said that Westerhousen "hath lain at the farm in the same room with her."

The governor told the court that "the passages concerning Mr. Westerhousen, and what is proved upon oath, yet not owned by him [leave] the court much unsatisfied." As to Westerhousen, this ambivalent declaration was the end of the case. He had been publicly embarrassed, but no punishment was ordered. The same could not be said of Meekes and Turner, who now became the focus of the court's attention.

The governor observed that the evidence before the court established that "beside the fornication, there hath been much impudence in lying, especially on his part, calling God to witness the truth of a thing which himself knew to be false, as he now professeth."

Before the court proceeded to sentence, Turner's stepfather, Goodanhousen, spoke up. He "desired the court to consider that Rebecka is weak and hath sore breasts and a froward child. . . . If it may be, they would spare corporal punishment and if they laid a fine, he would see it paid."

Hearing this, the court ordered that "Thomas Meekes be severely whipped for this folly of sinful uncleanness and for his lying and miscarriages that way [he was] fined 5 pounds." Turner was also sentenced to be whipped "if in reference to herself and child it may stand with due mercy." But "upon a view and search and a report made by the midwife and sister Kimberly, the court saw cause to forbear that and ordered her to pay a fine of 10 pounds, which Mr. Goodanhousen promised to pay for her."

This was on July 3, 1649. The records show that by September 4, 1649, Meekes and Turner had married.[4]

⊰⊱⊰⊱⊰

The Frisky Couple is the last significant case to be reported in the first volume of the records. It can hardly be said to constitute an inspiring finish to the General Court's first decade. Regardless of the court's strength in other areas, when it came to sexual matters, the theology and instincts of the General Court led to atrocious judicial actions.

The case of Meekes and Turner vividly displays the court's failings in this area. The subject matter of the inquiry is, from a modern point of view, bad enough. Meekes and Turner were not children. We learn at the end of the case that Turner already had a child. They were married within two months of the trial. Under these circumstances, a public judicial inquiry into their sexual relations deprived them (by modern standards) of their most intimate personal rights. The ultimate sentence of whipping (from which Turner was happily spared) increases the indignity. Beyond this, from a procedural point of view, the judicial excursion into Turner's supposed relationship with Westerhousen seems doubly pointless. Whether the inquiry was designed to humiliate Westerhousen (who had just emerged victorious in the Competing Claimants), Turner, or both, little justification for this excursion can now be found. The court was, presumably, attempting to make a public statement that scandalous behavior of this sort would not be tolerated. But in doing so, it underlined the fact that it was driven by theology at the expense of fairness to the various parties affected by its proceedings.

13

꘠꘠꘠

THE

RHODE ISLAND

PRIVATEER

꘠꘠꘠

The records of the New Haven Colony for the four years following 1649 have been lost for centuries.[1] When the records resume,
it is 1653. King Charles has lost his head, and the Protectorate
governs England. The governance of the New Haven Colony
has not been interrupted. Theophilus Eaton remains governor,
and John Davenport remains minister of the church. The New
Haven courts still meet, and many eventful cases await trial. The
first reported case on the docket of the Court of Magistrates is
the Case of the Rhode Island Privateer.

On July 1, 1653, Edward Hull was called before the court,
charged with "making a great disturbance at Milford, carrying it
in such a manner towards the jurisdiction and authority thereof
(at Milford) as is not to be borne." A written complaint by the
magistrate for Milford, William Fowler, was presented to the
court. The complaint described what appeared to be a theft from
a boat in Milford harbor. On closer examination, however, the
incident was anything but a routine larceny.

One Thomas Baxter owned the boat in question. Baxter was an Englishman who had "lived among the Dutch," possibly in the Dutch colony in New Amsterdam. During the First Anglo-Dutch War, fought from 1651 to 1653, the New England colonies considered the Dutch to be enemies. The New Haven Colony had seized Baxter's boat "for the service of the country" and also for a debt owed to Stephen Goodyear, the deputy governor of the colony and, as it happened, one of the four members of the Court of Magistrates hearing this very case.[2] Knowing this, Hull broke open the cabin of the boat, "took away a gun, a grappling iron, and some cordage, and carried it away." When a warrant was issued to appear before a Milford magistrate, Hull initially refused, saying he would come again shortly that way and make his answer. He did so "not long after," and when he appeared before the magistrate, he had the temerity "to justify what he had done."

Hull cited a "commission" given to him by the Rhode Island Colony. The evidence later submitted to the New Haven court makes it clear that this "commission" was "to take ... Dutch vessels, or such as are enemies to the Commonwealth of England." Hull was, it appears, a commissioned privateer. Standing before the magistrate, Hull was emphatic about the scope of his commission. "He broke out into many high words and threatening speeches ... that he might not only seize [the boat] but carry her away if he were able or else fire her or take away anything from her, and that any that should withstand him herein should answer it." When the magistrate demanded that he post security to come to a trial and answer for what he had done, Hull said "he hoped the rest of his company would come and set him at liberty and that he hoped the Dutch would come speedily and cut some of us off, and other threatening offensive words." Hull apparently was unable or unwilling to post security, so he was imprisoned while awaiting trial. During his imprisonment, he staged something of a hunger strike, drinking "nothing but sack and sugar."

When he appeared before the Court of Magistrates, Hull said, "It is true I seized the boat, but I first went to the Magistrate and told him that it was a prize." The "Magistrate" was apparently Magistrate Fowler of Milford, the very magistrate who subsequently signed the complaint bringing Hull before the court. According to Hull, "though it is true he heard [the boat] was seized for the country's use, yet the magistrate told him she was released." Fowler's subsequent complaint, however, denied that he had made such a statement, and Hull said he could not now prove it.

The court asked Hull what commission he had to do these things. He responded by showing his Rhode Island commission, which was read to the court. As mentioned, the commission was "to take ... Dutch vessels or such as are enemies to the Commonwealth of England." The New Haven court found "nothing ... therein to justify him in these carriages." Although Baxter had indeed "lived among the Dutch, yet now he hath deserted them." Under these circumstances, in the court's opinion, Baxter was not an "enemy."

"After sundry debates of this nature," the record continues, "the said Edward Hull and others that stood by saw that his commission would not bear him out in what he had done. Yet he continued in his justification, uttering some high words and offensive speeches before the Court. Whereupon the Court told him that if he justify himself in this and intends to proceed in such ways to the disturbance of the colonies, the Court must consider of another way than they yet thought of, that is to send him to England, to answer it there, and then he will see whether the Parliament will justify him in such courses as these and think him a fit man to be trusted with a commission which carries it in this manner to the Parliament's friends, thus to threaten them and hope that the Dutch, the Parliament's and our enemies, will speedily come and cut some of us off."

Hull "desired a little respite to consider" this judicial thunder-bolt. After a recess, Hull "quickly came before the Court again and acknowledged that by this debate with the Court he saw the compass of his commission more than ever he did before and doth see that he hath in this business gone beyond his commission and is very sorry for it and for giving out such speeches as he hath done in his haste and passion." He asked the court "to pass it by" and "promised to be more wary in attending his commission for time to come."

The court acknowledged Hull's professed change in attitude and pronounced itself "willing for this time to pass it by without any further trouble to him."

The court then turned to Ensign Alexander Bryan, who, it alleged, had assisted Hull in his taking of articles from the boat. When Bryan understood what Hull intended to do, the court said, "he did not acquaint the magistrate with it but countenanced him therein by going along with him." This made it appear as if Bryan approved of the action, although he knew that the boat had already been seized "for the country" and that "there was an attachment laid upon boat and goods for Mr. Goodyear for a particular debt." By doing this, according to the court, Bryan "himself became a surety that the boat and goods should be safely preserved for Mr. Goodyear's use." This "carriage in respect of the public," Bryan was told, was "contrary to his oath of fidelity taken to the jurisdiction."

Bryan acknowledged that all of these things were true "and confessed it was his great fault so to do, and had he considered his way, he should have done otherwise."

The Milford deputies who were prosecuting the case advised the court that, under these circumstances, a warning would be sufficient. Considering this prosecutorial request and Bryan's own acknowledgment of fault, the court "passed it by without any further trouble to him at present."

⬧⬧⬧⬧⬧

The Case of the Rhode Island Privateer says much about the political environment of the New England colonies in the early 1650s. The New Haven Colony had necessarily acknowledged the fact that the mother country, now under the Protectorate, was at war with the Dutch. The seizure of Baxter's boat "for the country" suggests that the colony was taking at least symbolic effort to take part in that war. But it now had to deal with the fact that another colony, Rhode Island, was commissioning privateers to seize Dutch boats in the harbors of New Haven Colony.

Jurisprudentially, the case is teeming with meaty issues. In an era long predating the Constitution, what deference should one colony afford a commission of privateering issued by another colony? Assuming that some general deference should be shown, how did the Rhode Island commission apply to the tricky facts presented here? The boat had been seized "for the service of the country," but it was also the subject of a private attachment for a debt owed to Goodyear.

Hull apparently knew these facts in advance. Even if Baxter, the boat's owner, was himself associated with the enemy, how could the boat be subject to a seizure by a privateer after it had *already* been seized "for the country"? Was Baxter associated with the enemy in the first place? We are told that he had lived with the Dutch but subsequently deserted them. On the other hand, assuming the boat itself was not subject to legal seizure by a privateer, how can we say that Hull acted less than lawfully? He had, after all, secured the approval of a magistrate for his seizure prior to the event. Ensign Bryan, an official of the local jurisdiction, accompanied Hull. These are the careful and conservative actions of a law-abiding citizen, not the hallmarks of criminal intent. Finally, why didn't Magistrate Goodyear recuse himself? The boat had been attached for a debt owed to him. Wasn't the case decided by a judge with a direct financial interest in the case? A proper consideration of these issues would be a huge judicial task.

As we can see, this was anything but a routine larceny case. It was, instead, a big mess. The court decided to cut the Gordian knot in a way familiar to judges of any age. It blustered and threatened and, having gained an acknowledgment of wrongdoing, let the defendant (and Ensign Bryan as well) off with a warning. A modern judge looking to resolve a difficult case occasionally looks for a resolution that will allow each party to declare victory and move on. This is what happened here. The court obtained acknowledgments of wrongdoing by both Hull and Bryan. It also avoided having to resolve the many legal issues presented by the case—a substantial institutional benefit to a busy court. Hull and Bryan avoided punishment and got to move on with their lives. Each side could look at the outcome and declare victory. From a doctrinal point of view, this was imperfect justice, for it left many questions unanswered. It was, however, practical justice, acceptable to the parties.

Whether there was practical justice for the various claimants to the boat is more difficult to determine. Who ended up owning the boat? On this question, the record is conspicuously silent.

14

≈≋≈

THE REPUTED

WITCH

≈≋≈

On August 4, 1653, Elizabeth Godman came before the Court of Magistrates with an unusual case.[1] She was reputed to be a witch, and she wanted to be exonerated. The court, however, examined her claim and found that Godman brought her reputation on herself.

Godman's case appears to be what we would now call a defamation action, although the court was a court without lawyers and didn't require exact legal phrasing. Godman came to court with an accusation against Goodwife Larremore. (We don't know Larremore's first name.) According to Godman, Larremore had seen her at the house of Jeremy Whitnel and said of Godman, "So soon as I saw her, I thought of a witch." Godman didn't claim any damages for Larremore's statement (which she would have to do in a modern defamation action), but she apparently wanted her reputation restored.

Larremore responded that she had "spoken to that purpose" at the house of William Hooke but not at the house of Jeremy Whitnel. She had made her statement at Hooke's house because John Davenport, the minister of the New Haven Church, had spoken of witches at about that time and "showed that a froward, discontented frame of spirit was a subject fit for the Devil to work upon in that way, and she looked upon Mrs. Godman to be of such a frame of spirit."

Godman replied that Whitnel's maid could testify as to Larremore's statement. The maid was duly sent for. When the maid appeared, she testified that she heard Godman and Larremore talking. She thought she heard Larremore say she "thought of a witch in the Bay when she sees Mrs. Godman." Larremore added that Godman had her appear before the governor for this. The governor asked her if she thought Godman was a witch, and she answered no.

The court told Godman that Larremore wasn't the first person she'd brought before the court for calling her a witch. Godman had made similar accusations against an impressive array of people: Mr. and Mrs. Goodyear, Mr. and Mrs. Hooke, Mrs. Bishop, Mrs. Atwater, Mary Miles (Mrs. Atwater's maid), Hannah and Elizabeth Lamberton, and Goodwife Thorpe. Godman replied that all of these people "had given out speeches that made folks think she was a witch." She charged Mrs. Atwater "to be the cause of all." To "clear things," she asked if someone could read a "writing." The "writing" was a report of an examination before a magistrate held in May 1653, where Godman had more fully stated her accusations against Atwater. "Sundry of the passages in the writing" were then read.

The Magistrate's Examination

The report of the magistrate's examination of Godman's complaints occupies several pages of the New Haven Colony records. Godman told the magistrate that each of the various people she accused had "suspected her for a witch." The magistrate then considered these allegations in detail.

Godman was first asked about her accusations against the Hookes. She said she heard "they had something against her about their son."

Hooke replied that he was "not without fears" and had reason for them. He first became suspicious because Godman was "shut out at Mr. Atwater's upon suspicion." He had been "troubled in his sleep about witches" when his boy was sick "in a very strange manner." He looked upon Godman "as a malicious one." She would often be speaking about witches and would rather justify them than condemn them. She said, "Why do they provoke them? Why do they not let them come into the church?" On another occasion, she was speaking about witches and said that if they accused her for a witch, she would have them to the governor. She would trounce them. On a third occasion, she said, she had some thoughts about what she would do if the devil should come to suck her, and she resolved he should not suck her. In addition to these comments, Hooke said that whatever was done in the church meetings, she should know it presently and she could not give an adequate explanation for her knowledge.

Hooke's wife, Jane Hooke, agreed that Godman (whom she called "Mrs. Elzebeth") "could tell sundry things that was done at the church meeting before meeting was done."

A Native American named Time (described in the records as "Mr. Hooke's Indian") said that "in church meeting time, she would go out and come in again and tell them what was done at meeting." Godman would not tell Time who told her, and Time asked her, "Did not the Devil tell you?"

Henry Boutle and "some others" accused Godman of "talking and muttering to herself."

Time said he heard Godman talking to herself one time and asked her, "Who talk you to?" Godman responded, "To you." Time replied, "You talk to the Devil." Godman, however, "made nothing of it."

Hooke said he had heard that "they that are addicted that way would hardly be kept away from the houses where they do mischief." So it was with Godman. When Hooke's boy was sick, she would not be kept away from him, nor would she go away once she was there. One time, Mrs. Hooke told her to go away and thrust her from the boy, but she turned again and said she would "look on him."

Mrs. Goodyear said that one time she questioned Godman about the boy's sickness and said, "What think you of him? Is he not strangely handled?" Godman replied, "What? Do you think he is bewitched?" Goodyear responded, "Nay. I will keep my thoughts to myself, but in time God will discover."

Someone (we don't know who) told the magistrate that "it is suspicious that she hath put the boy's sickness upon some other cause, as that he had turned his brains with sliding, and said the boy would be well again, though he was handled in such a strange manner as the doctor said he had not met with the like."

Goodyear said that he asked Godman if she was not the cause of his disease. Godman denied it but in an unconvincing way.

Hooke further said that when Mr. Bishop was married, Godman came into his house so troubled he thought this might be from some affection to Bishop. Hooke asked Godman if this was so, and she said "yes." It was suspicious that as soon as the Bishops were contacted, Mrs. Bishop fell into very strange fits that had continued to that time. There was much suspicion that Godman had been the cause of the loss of Mrs. Bishop's children, for she could tell when Mrs. Bishop was going to be ill. Godman has given out that Mrs. Bishop killed her children with longing because she longs for everything she sees; Mrs. Bishop denied this. When Godman was required to give an instance, she said that, according to Mrs. Hooke, Mrs. Bishop longed for some peace. Mrs. Hooke, however, reported that Godman had said Mrs. Bishop was much given to longing, and that was the reason she lost her children.

"Another thing suspicious" about Godman, according to the records, was that she could tell that Mrs. Atwater had figs in her pocket when she saw none of them. Godman responded that she smelled them and could smell figs if she came in the room near persons that had them. This answer, however, was tested by a classic courtroom trick. Mrs. Atwater came near Godman with figs in her pocket, and Godman failed to smell them. (Whether or not Atwater's figs were ripe is not recorded.)

Mrs. Atwater additionally said that one time Godman could tell they had pease porridge (baked split pea pudding) when none of them could tell how she came to know. When asked, Godman said that she saw it on the table. Another time Godman said she was there in the morning when the maid was preparing the porridge. Further, the night the figs were spoken of they had strangers to dinner, and Godman was at their house. Godman "cut a sop" (i.e., ate bread that was dipped in soup or juices) and put it in the pan. Betty Brewster called the maid and told her Godman was about her works of darkness. That night, Brewster was in a most miserable case, hearing a most dreadful noise, which put her in great fear and trembling and a great sweat. In the morning, she looked as one who had been almost dead. Mrs. Atwater told Godman of her suspicions and warned Godman not to come to her house, yet Godman came again the next night for beer.

Godman accused Mr. Goodyear of asking her to come when Mrs. Bishop was in a sore fit, to check on her, and of saying he feared Mrs. Bishop was a witch. Mrs. Goodyear became exceedingly angry and asked the servants to tell her who had bewitched her, for she was not well. At this point, Hannah Lamberton, being in the room, fell into a very sore fit in a very strange manner.

Mrs. Goodyear told the magistrate a somewhat different story. She and her daughter had gone to Godman and told her that some thought they were bewitched. Referring to Mrs. Bishop, they said, "Here is a poor weak woman. What think you of her? Some have thought she is bewitched." Godman laughed and said, "Alas, who should bewitch her? She had a cousin was so." Mrs. Goodyear replied that "if there be any such persons, God would find them out and discover them, for I never knew a witch die in their bed." Godman responded, "You mistake, for a great many die and go to the grave in an orderly way."

On another occasion, Mrs. Goodyear reported that she said to Godman, "What think you of my daughter's case?" Godman replied, "What, do you think I have bewitched her?" Mrs. Goodyear responded, "If you be the party, look to it, for they intend to have such as is suspected before the magistrate."

Godman accused Hannah Lamberton of saying that Godman "lay for somewhat to suck her." This happened when she came in hot one day, undressed partially, and lay down on the bed in her room.

Lamberton said that this happened when she and her sister Elizabeth went up into the garret above her room and looked down and said, "Look how she lies. She lies as if somebody was sucking her." Upon that, Godman arose and said, "Yes, yes, so there is." Lamberton said, "She has something there," for it seemed as if something was under the clothes. Godman denied that there was anything under her clothes and threatened Lamberton. About two days later, Lamberton's fits began. One night, she had an especially dreadful fit; she was pinched and heard a hideous noise, and she was in a strange manner sweating and burning and at one point was cold and so full of pain that she shrieked.

Elizabeth Lamberton said that one time children came down and said that Godman was talking to herself, and they were afraid. She went up softly and heard Godman talk, saying, "Will you fetch me some beer? Will you go? Will you go?"

Henry Boutele reported that one morning about break of day, he heard Godman talk to herself, as if somebody was with her.

The magistrate's examination continued to a second day. John Davenport, the minister of the New Haven Church, now joined the magistrate.

The magistrate asked Godman why she had said that Mrs. Bishop longed for almost everything she sees and, when she could not have it, that was the cause of her fainting fits and the loss of her children. Godman replied that she had heard something from Mrs. Hooke to that purpose, that Mrs. Bishop longed for pease pudding.

Mrs. Hooke was sent for. When she arrived, she denied ever saying this. Jane Hooke (it is unclear if this was a different person than Mrs. Hooke) said Godman had told her that Mrs. Bishop was much given to longing, and that was the reason she lost her children.

Hannah Lamberton said that Godman had told her so as well.

Mrs. Bishop said that another woman in town told her she had heard Godman say as much, so she could not deny it. Bishop was told that Godman had much inquired after the time of her delivery of her children and would speak of it so that Mrs. Goodyear and her daughters marveled how she could know. Hannah Lamberton one time told her mother that Godman "kept her sister's count" (i.e., kept track of her sister's children). When asked the reason for this, Godman could give no reason. When told that she had slandered Mrs. Bishop, Godman said she could say nothing "but must lie under it" (i.e., stick to her story).

Mrs. Goodyear said that when Mrs. Atwater's kinswoman was married, Mrs. Bishop was there, and, the room being hot, she was "something faint." Upon that, Godman said she would have many of these fainting fits after she was married. Godman also said that Mrs. Bishop had such fits as a child.

Godman said she didn't remember these remarks. When asked her reason for making them, she could not give a reason.

Goodwife Thorpe complained that Godman came to her house and asked to buy some chickens. Thorpe said she had none to sell. When Godman had gone away, Thorpe thought that if Godman was what folks suspected her to be, she might hurt Thorpe's chickens. Quickly after, one chicken died. Thorpe remembered that if chickens were bewitched, they would waste away internally. She opened the chicken, and its gizzard was filled with water and worms. She had never before seen a hen or a chicken in such a bad state. Other chickens have since gone missing and are likely dead. Thorpe thought it would be good to explain this so it could be considered with the other things.

Back to the Trial

After "sundry passages" of the magistrate's examination had been read, Godman resumed her attack on Mrs. Atwater. According to Godman, Mrs. Atwater had said she thought Godman was a witch and that Hobbamocke (a Native spirit thought by colonists to be the devil) was her husband. But although Godman had been warned ahead of time to have her witnesses ready, she had no witnesses to offer in proof of her claims.

Godman was then asked if the contents of the magistrate's examination did not give all who heard them a just ground of suspicion that she was indeed a witch. Godman confessed that they did but said if she spoke the things reported by Mr. Hooke, she was not herself. The court responded that she need not say if she spoke the things in question, for she had before the governor and many witnesses confessed them all as her words, though she made the same excuse that she was not in a right mind.

Mrs. Hooke now testified that Godman was in a sober frame and spoke in a deliberate way, as she ordinarily does.

Godman was also reminded of testimony before the governor that Mr. Goodyear had fallen into a swooning fit after he had spoken something one night in the exposition of a chapter she liked not. As soon as Goodyear had finished she flung out of the room in a discontented way and cast a fierce look at Goodyear as she went out. Immediately, Goodyear (who had been well before) fell into a swoon. Several witnesses affirmed that she had left the room when this happened.

After considering these matters, the court declared to Godman that she had unjustly accused the several persons before named, since she could prove nothing against them. The court added that "her carriage [behavior] doth justly render her suspicious of witchcraft, which she herself in so many words confesseth." Therefore, the court wished her to be careful of her behavior in the future , for if further proof came, these events would not be forgotten. It therefore charged her not to go in an offensive way to folks' houses in a railing manner as it seemed she had done but to keep her place and meddle with her own business. With that admonition, Godman's effort to clear her name in court ended ignominiously.

⹂⹂⹂

This remarkable case has obvious overtones of the famous witchcraft trials held in Salem forty years later and of other instances of mass hysteria, from the Holland Tulip Mania of 1637 to the Communist witch hunts of the 1950s, that have recurred throughout human history. As far as the records indicate, a substantial number of New Haven colonists in 1653 simply took leave of their senses. This was true both of the ordinary people who literally went into fits when crossing paths with a suspected witch and of the possibly more educated New Haven magistrates who heard such testimony without a trace of skepticism. As Arthur Miller knew when he wrote *The Crucible*, this credulity is not a characteristic limited to ignorant people of long ago. The Case of the Reputed Witch says something about all of us.

Our condemnation of these proceedings, however, should be tempered with a tiny allotment of praise. While the Salem judges, like their judicial counterparts in seventeenth-century England, hanged witches, the New Haven Colony did not.[2] Elizabeth Godman left the New Haven Magistrates Court disgraced but alive.

The New Haven Colony, like Salem, was far from idiosyncratic in its fear of witchcraft. The English authorities had persecuted suspected witches at least since Elizabethan times, and there was an intense period of persecution during the English Civil War when England executed at least a hundred persons found to be witches.[3] A century later, even the renowned legal commentator,

William Blackstone, was inclined to hedge his bets by writing that "in general there has been such a thing as witchcraft, though one cannot give credit to any particular modern instance of it."[4]

In legal terms, Godman was never charged with being a witch, and the court never found her to be one. It instead admonished her to refrain from suspicious conduct. The New Haven magistrates were plainly eager to avoid a finding of witchcraft, which might leave them no alternative to imposing the death penalty. While the Reputed Witch leaves us profoundly disturbed at the court's gullibility (not to mention saddened at the human condition), we can be modestly thankful that Elizabeth Godman was allowed to live.

15

·✦✦✦·

THE MILFORD
BESTIALITY CASE

·✦✦✦·

When the New Haven Colony records were first printed from the original manuscript sources in the late 1850s, some cases involving the prosecution of sexual crimes were "deemed unfit for publication."[1] This veil of decorum is inconvenient to the modern historian. As with other trials, the trials of sexual offenses provide a window into both judicial and social history. By studying such cases, we not only see the official operations of the court but also gain an intimate perspective of the everyday lives of ordinary people.

The original manuscripts survive in the Connecticut State Archives. By consulting them,[2] it is possible to fill in the gaps in the printed volumes. This brings us to the first case omitted in the printed records: the Milford Bestiality Case.

On February 2, 1655, Walter Robinson, a fifteen-year-old apprentice, was called before the Court of Magistrates and told that he stood charged with "committing that horrible sin of bestiality, with a bitch, and therein abasing the nature of man in a most filthy way, and that upon the Lord's day." The court did not hear witnesses. It instead read a written report of evidence heard by two deputies of the court in Milford the previous autumn. Those records told the following story.

On November 29, 1654, Edward Willson, a seaman, testified under oath before Deputy Benjamin Fenn. Willson stated that on November 18, 1654, he had seen Robinson, an apprentice to a Mr. Fowler of Milford, with a bitch while Robinson was watching sheep. Robinson had taken the bitch by the hind parts and worked with his body standing toward the bitch. Willson called to Robinson that he would be hanged for his offense. Robinson let go of the bitch, looked at his "member," and ran away.

Robinson was then brought in for examination before Deputy Fenn. He confessed that he was the boy described by Willson and that the incident had occurred on a holy day. He admitted to holding the dog toward him. He heard Willson call out, "Sirrah, if you look fairly, you will be hanged for it," after which he looked at his member. He had run away as fast as he could. He denied that any other misconduct had occurred.

On December 5, 1654, a second Milford deputy, Robert Treat, further examined Robinson. Robinson "owned all that he had confessed before." He also confessed that "he did intend to have done more," but he had stopped when the seaman called out.

Deputy Treat reminded Robinson "of his impudent and notorious lying." Treat ordered him imprisoned in the marshal's house because of "other filthy and corrupting carriages at Milford." Treat further informed Robinson that he had already confessed to Deputy Fenn and that he should "now in a more public way confess his sin and give glory to God."

Robinson took the hint. He told the deputy that on the afternoon in question, he had gone to a park in Milford. Another boy was there with a bitch. Robinson called the bitch to him. He took the dog by its hind legs and pulled down his clothing. Taking his member in his hand, with the purpose of unnatural copulation, he "put it in a little way into the bitch's body." He did not, however, "enter her body so far as he might have done," because the seaman called out to him that he would be hanged. "Feeling some grumbling pain in his member, he looked upon it." He then ran away. He was afraid after he had done it that he would be hanged.

Robinson's fear was well founded. Having read the evidence of the Milford deputies, the court proceeded to announce its sentence. It declared that Robinson's "sin is such as by the law of God and the law of this jurisdiction, he ought to die." It would pronounce this sentence "that all others may hear and fear and take warning not to commit such wickedness." The sentence of death was to be executed upon Robinson by hanging on the gallows, and "the bitch which hath committed this horrible wickedness be killed in his sight at that time." The sentence was ordered to be carried out on the first Wednesday in March, "so that in the meantime he may consider his sin and repent and seek to God in Christ, that mercy may be showed to his poor soul."

The Milford Bestiality Case evokes both sadness and outrage. The sadness is for Walter Robinson, a fifteen-year-old boy filled more with hormones than with judgment. Guilty of an undoubtedly inappropriate act—an act that would likely prompt a modern court to order counseling—he was turned in by a bystander, pressured by the authorities to confess, and hanged following a mockery of a trial.

The case offends modern sensibilities not because of its sexual details but because of its abandonment of basic notions of justice. The outrage is for the judicial system that produced this result. Bestiality was a capital offense in England as well as in the New Haven Colony at the time, and the English and New Haven courts of this period were perfectly capable of hanging children. But the court sentencing Robinson to death did so entirely on the basis of a written record, with no witnesses, no counsel, no jury, and as far as the record indicates, no opportunity for the defendant to speak on his own behalf. This would be considered an outrage even in seventeenth-century England.

16

❧❧❧

THE
BOAT SEX
CASE

❧❧❧

In the spring of 1655, a complaint reached the Court of Magistrates that sexual impropriety had occurred between William Ellit and Hannah Spencer on a boat traveling from Milford to Stamford.[1] On May 28, the two miscreants were brought before the court and charged with "unclean, filthy carriages." The owner of the boat, William Benfeild, was brought before the court as well. As it inquired as to what exactly had happened on the boat, the court heard a variety of stories.

Spencer began by telling the court that she had done whatever it was she had done (what exactly this was remained unspecified) because Ellit had "forced" her. Ellit denied this, whereupon Spencer began to speak in greater detail.

Spencer declared that she took a passage in Benfeild's boat to go from Milford to Stamford one night. She was in the cuddy (a small cabin in a boat), and Benfeild sat by the door. Ellit came in and "asked her if she would have him." Spencer replied that "it was not in her power. She was at the dispose [control] of the church at Milford." At this, Ellit "fell upon her and by degrees got up her coats and had carnal knowledge of her, but without her consent." Spencer said, however, that this happened when Benfeild was in the cuddy with them. The three of them were lying close by each other, with Spencer in the middle.

Ellit, who had previously denied everything, now changed his story. He confessed that "he had had carnal knowledge of her, but not by force but with her consent." The details of Ellit's story differed markedly from Spencer's. "He had endeavored it that time she speaks of in the boat but could not. But in the morning, while the boat was sailing, he was at the helm and, being cold, asked Benfeild to take the helm. He went into the cuddy with her, and she spake as pitying of him, saying he shaked with cold, and he lay down by her and then with her consent did it, but forced her not."

Spencer replied that Ellit's story was not true. "It was but one time, and that was in the night when Benfeild was in the cuddy."

The court asked Spencer, "How could that be a forced act, when another lay close by and saith he cannot tell that any such thing was done, nor did hear her cry out? Only one time [Benfeild] did hear her say with a mild voice, 'William Ellit, let me alone.'"

A new witness, Gregory Taylor of Stamford now appeared. Taylor told the court that he had been in the boat and, because his wife was sick, was kept awake all night. He heard no crying out, which "she would have done had not her consent been gained." Taylor further testified that Spencer had "carried it pleasingly" to Ellit afterward, and as both confessed, they "fell into a treaty of marriage in Benefeild's [sic] presence . . . and agreed to be married at Greenwich." When Spencer arrived at Stamford, however, "she was unwilling, having heard by the wife of John Graden, a Dutchman, that Ellit [had told John Graden] that he had got a sweetheart who was an ugly creature, but she had a good portion [dowry], and when he had got that, he would give her a kick." John Graden affirmed that he had heard this statement.

At this point, the court called Benfeild before it and told him that he was "charged with several miscarriages."[2] First, he violated his trust to Spencer, a passenger in his boat, by negligently suffering her chastity to be violated. Second, "he himself had in a filthy way touched her naked body." Benfeild interposed that this was "accidental," but the court replied that "it doth not so appear, he having boasted of this with other filthy passages to the seamen in Mr. Mayo's vessel." Third, the court continued, Benfeild had "suffered Ellit a second time (knowing of their filthiness the night before) to go into the cuddy alone with Hannah Spencer, and there to have opportunity to do so wickedly." Fourth, "he had allowed of a treaty of marriage in his boat . . . without consent of parents or any which had the dispose of her."

Benfeild first denied these charges but afterward confessed that "the things were true." He was ashamed "for his sinful words in Mr. Mayo's vessel." He confessed that "he should have been more careful of his trust and not have suffered such treaties of marriage, especially with William Ellit, whom he knew to be naught, though for want of other help was forced to make use of him in that voyage."

Having heard the evidence, the court proceeded to sentence the individuals before it.

The court first considered the case of William Ellit. It stated that "though they find no satisfying evidence that it was a forced rape, yet it is a heinous filthiness, and it likely was begun in a way of force though after her consent might be drawn. But, as fornication, it is a great sin and folly in a high degree and severely to be punished. Beside [the court found] his enticing to marriage, with a purpose declared that after he had got her portion, he would give her a kick."

For his "filthiness," Ellit was sentenced "to be severely whipped." For the additional offense of "enticing her to marriage without consent of those who had the dispose of her," he was ordered to pay a fine of forty shillings. The court ordered that Ellit "bear all charges the jurisdiction hath been put to about this business and remain a prisoner til this sentence be fulfilled."

The court next dealt with Hannah Spencer. The tribunal explained that it "looks upon her miscarriages as great, though they conceive she hath been drawn by corruption and temptation, yet they cannot but judge that she deserves to be severely corrected." But "considering the weakness of her body (which is more than ordinary)," the court ordered Spencer to pay a fine of ten pounds to the jurisdiction and that "she be present at the whipping post when Ellit receives his correction, that she may in some measure bear the shame of her sin."

The court finally turned to William Benfeild. It found that "he did not at first attend his trust in looking to Hannah Spencer as he ought, and for giving an opportunity a second time for Ellit to perfect his filthiness, [that he spoke] filthy, base words, such as himself saith he is ashamed to name before the court, aboard Mr. Mayo's vessel, and that he would be a witness of and a persuader to a marriage to be accomplished betwixt them, without consent of those which had the dispose of her."

For these acts, Benfeild was sentenced to pay a fine of five pounds. At this point, for reasons unexplained by the record,

Ensign Alexander Bryan (whom we met in the Case of the Rhode Island Privateer) entered the case. Bryan agreed to pay this sum on Benfeild's behalf.

❦

It is impossible to determine what actually happened in William Benfeild's boat on that spring evening of long ago. The court found that the allegation of forcible rape was not supported by "satisfying evidence." Given the passage of time and the conflicting stories presented, it is difficult to fault the court's conclusion. The evidence that Ellit and Spencer entered into a "treaty of marriage" subsequently dissolved when Spencer learned of Ellit's unkind words, suggests that the sexual encounter between them may well have been a consensual act later characterized as a criminal act in the aftermath of a lovers' quarrel. Of course, we cannot know this for sure. Perhaps Spencer felt she had no choice but to marry Ellit after he had forcibly raped her. All we can say is that the evidence supporting either conclusion is less than "satisfying."

There are certainly questions that we would like to ask. Were Ellit and Spencer strangers when they boarded Benfeild's boat, or did they have a preexisting relationship? Was Spencer a minor? (Ellit's remarks to Graden suggest that Ellit was an a grown man seeking to take advantage of his new "sweetheart.") What did Spencer mean when she told Ellit that "it was not in her power" to consent to his advances because "she was at the dispose of the church at Milford"? Did the Milford church have control over her because of her age or the "good portion" that Ellit coveted, or did it have such power over all unmarried females in its congregation? We know that the court took this power of the church seriously because it specifically mentioned this consideration in sentencing Benfeild.

The court's legal view, however, rendered such questions unnecessary. Any sexual encounter between unmarried persons—regardless of their relationship, status, or consent—was "fornication" and categorically prohibited. This was a crime punishable by the public whipping of both parties. Only the "weakness" of Spencer's body saved her from Ellit's fate. The court's eventual punishment of the parties had a special note of cruelty—Spencer was forced to be present while Ellit was whipped so "that she may in some measure bear the shame of her sin." If Ellit and Spencer were former lovers, this punishment was bad enough. If Ellit had committed a forcible rape, this treatment of his victim was outrageous beyond description. In either event, this was the New Haven version of Hester Prynne's scarlet letter.

Another principle accepted by the court is worth noting. Benfeild, the owner of the boat, was viewed as holding a position of trust with respect to his passengers. He had an obligation to protect Spencer from sexual abuse, and his failure to do so was considered "negligence." The court was obviously focusing on sexual propriety, and we cannot be sure that the court would have imposed the same standard of care if Spencer had tripped on an oar negligently left on deck. But the suggestion that passengers on a ship were entitled to some form of legal protection and that the owner of a public conveyance has an obligation to protect the safety of his passengers was a surprisingly modern one by a seventeenth-century court.

17

THE YOUTH

SEX CASES

✥✥✥✥✥

May 28, 1655, was a major day for sex cases in the Court of Magistrates.[1] On the same day that the court heard the Boat Sex
Case, it heard a series of interrelated sexual misconduct cases
involving five young people employed by William Judson. The
nineteenth-century printer of the records heavily censored the
Youth Sex Cases, and the account here is largely taken from the
manuscript sources.

The first case, the trial of John Knight, was an extremely serious
case involving the sexual assault of a child. On May 28, 1655, after
the conclusion of the Boat Sex Case, Knight was called before the
court and "charged with committing filthiness in a sodomitical way
with Peter Vincon, his master Judson's boy, of the age of fourteen
years or somewhat more." Knight denied that he "had committed
any such filthiness." The court then read the testimony of two witnesses, Thomas and Samuel Richards, taken before the governor
on May 17, 1655. The witnesses were in court and affirmed their
previous testimony to be true.

The witnesses had testified before the governor that they were
going on a path about a mile beyond the river when they saw John

Knight and Peter, Goodman Judson's boy, together. The boy's head and shoulders were upon the ground, and his legs were drawn up under Knight's arms. Knight was moving his body in such a manner that indicated they were committing "filthiness together." The witnesses went on toward them and observed as closely as they could. The boy was upon the ground, and Knight stood behind him. As they apprehended, Knight had a "guilty countenance." The witnesses said nothing but went on their way.

Samuel Richards further told the governor that before they encountered Knight, "he heard them groaning." He looked at them and quickly left.

After this testimony had been read, Peter Vincon was called to relate what Knight had done to him. Vincon said that, as John Knight and he were keeping their master's cattle beyond the east river, Knight said to him, "What play shall we play?" Vincon said, "No play." But Knight came to him, took his legs under his arms and drew up his breeches to his body. Knight pulled out his member and would have put it into his body. Vincon refused, but Knight said it would not hurt him. Vincon said, no matter, he should not. After the young men (presumably the Richards) went by, Knight threw him down and again pulled out his member. Knight would have put it into his body, but he would not let him.

Vincon further said that one time before this, when they were keeping their cattle in a swamp, Knight threw him down and pulled down his breeches and would have entered his body.

Knight was asked what he said to the charge. He said it was not true.

The court told Knight that he had confessed to Mr. Hooke that he had the boy's legs under his arms and that the two witnesses had affirmed what he had formerly admitted and what he now impudently denied. Knight responded that it was true that he had the boy's legs up, but it was to push him, which, the records report, "the Court would not believe."

The court's attention now turned to Knight's relationship with Mary Clarke. The court asked him "what filthy carriages he is guilty of toward Mary Clarke, his master's maidservant?" Knight replied, "None at all." In response, the court called Clarke before it, along with her parents.

The court asked Clarke what Knight had done to her. Clarke, however, was reluctant to speak, so her mother was called "to declare to the court what her daughter had told her that John Knight had done to her."

Goodwife Clarke replied that her daughter Mary had told her Knight had "several times, three or four times at least, abused her in a filthy way, discovering her nakedness" and touching her with his body. She would cry out when he did this. The first time, she told Goodman [Judson] and his wife about it and prayed they would "put John Knight away." Also she, Goodwife Clarke, would take away her daughter. The Judsons promised that Knight and Mary Clarke would not be together alone, and they would be mindful of her. This promise was not performed. Knight went to Hartford for some time, but then he returned. But now a little before he was taken into custody, and after Goodman Judson had promised they wouldn't be together for more than half an hour, on the same day "he let them be in the fields together." Knight "came to her, threw her down upon her belly, and lay upon her base parts," with her skirt[2] pulled up. Then, "in a filthy way," Knight "spilt his seed" on her skirt, a mark she noticed after she stood up.

The court asked Knight what he said to this charge. Knight said he never did any of this to her.

Goodman Judson and Goodwife Clarke replied that they had dealt on numerous occasions with Knight about his filthy behavior toward Mary Clarke and that he had admitted[3] these charges and promised amendment. Knight did not deny this.

The court asked Peter Vincon what he had seen in John Knight's behavior toward Mary Clarke. Vincon said that one time in the second quarter, they were together, and Knight threw her down and would have done something to her, but she beat him off and said she would tell her "dame" (Goodman Judson's wife). ("Which she did," Goody Judson interposed.) Another time, in the barn, when she came to give the cattle meals and they were husking corn, he threw her down, kissed her, and rolled around with her in the barn. He would have done something to her with his member. She said she would tell her master (Goodman Judson). Several times when his master and dame had gone to bed, Knight pulled her to his knee, kissed her, rolled her around, and put his hand under her skirt. Another time in the meadow, he would tumble about and play with her, and she would not be quiet for him.

Knight denied all this and said the boy wronged him.

After this, the court heard that Mary Clarke had said she would tell something of Knight that would hang him. The court examined her and asked if John Knight had entered her body. She replied no, but he attempted it and laid down on her naked body. He would have entered but could not, though he hurt her by trying to do it with his hand. He ejaculated on her naked body.

The court asked Clarke why she didn't confess these things to Magistrate Francis Newman when he examined her; Newman had asked her about some filthy behavior of Jonathan Coventry toward her, and she was asked what she knew of John Knight regarding this type of behavior and she said nothing. Clarke responded that the reason was her dame told her to say nothing of John Knight.

Goodwife Judson would not deny this but said she told Clarke this because she thought Knight had enough upon him already. The court was unsatisfied with this answer and told Goodwife Judson that she (in a sinful way, for ends of her own) tried to conceal it, yet God in another way brought it to light.

Having heard this evidence, the court confronted the individuals before it.

Mary Clarke's parents were told they were exceedingly to blame; despite knowing what a filthy fellow John Knight was before with Francis Hall's children and being now informed that he had begun this way of filthiness with their daughter, they let her stay with the Judsons and did not complain about Knight to public authority. The Clarkes said they intended to do this, but Goodman Judson had promised that Knight should go away and while he was there they should not be together.

Goodman Judson and his wife were told that they had "done exceeding ill" by concealing these things from public authority. This was especially so since they knew John Knight for what he was and how "near death" (i.e., close to receiving the death penalty) he was before for "filthiness" such as this; Knight had been punished and worn a halter, although thanks to Goodman Judson's intervention, the halter had been taken off. They had neglected their trust and duty toward Mary Clarke and her parents, allowing Knight and Clarke to be alone together, thereby giving him opportunity both to abuse and to corrupt her, contrary to their promise to her parents. They had not only concealed it themselves but counseled Mary Clarke to conceal it also, all of which renders them very guilty.

The Judsons said they endeavored to keep Knight and Clarke apart. But, the court noted, it was testified by several people that the two had been often together alone, in the meadows, in the woods, in the cornfields, and two or three times in the barn husking corn, of which things Goodman Judson could not clear himself.

These things being largely and fully debated, the court took them into serious consideration. The court remembered John Knight's former behavior with the children of Francis Hall, a "loathsome filthiness." Having consulted with the elders of the jurisdiction concerning John Knight's miscarriages in all the afore-mentioned particulars, it was evident to them that he was a lewd, profane, filthy, corrupting, incorrigible person and a notorious liar; with the sodomitical attempt just proved, and other filthy, defiling ways, he was seen as a destructive person. This had gone on time after time, so that there seemed to be no end of his "filthiness." The court thought that nothing would help him, whether public punishment or private warning. The court did not think him fit to live among men and so sentenced Knight to be put to death by hanging on the gallows.

After this sentence, Knight confessed, both to the marshal and others, that all that Mary Clarke charged him with was true, but he denied what Peter Vincon had charged him with, in reference to sodomitical filthiness.

The court now turned to Mary Clarke. It looked upon her as woefully corrupted by John Knight, as seen by her own confession alongside other evidence given. She had gone along with him too much, and so a filthy disposition had arisen in her. The court therefore ordered that she be severely whipped, to see if it would please God to bless the stripes and work out this sinful folly.

For Goodman Judson and his wife, the court considered their breach of trust and promise in giving Knight such opportunities to be alone with Clarke, although they knew of his past and present "filthy disposition." The Judsons had concealed this from public authority when they first knew of Knight's behavior, and so his sin continued. God's wrath might have broken out against the place for the same. In fact, his wife counseled Clarke to conceal it when she was examined, so that much of this mischief had come by their neglect. For this, William Judson was ordered to pay ten pounds as a fine to the jurisdiction, so that it would be a warning to governors of families to be more careful and watchful over the charge and trust they take upon them.

For Peter Vincon, because he had been instrumental in this filthy way with John Knight, as he now confessed, three times, and because he concealed it and stiffly denied it at his first examination before the governor, the court ordered him to be whipped, as a warning to him and other boys to take heed not to fall into such behavior again.

The Youth Sex Cases were not finished. The court, having heard of "some unclean carriages betwixt Jonathan Coventry, Thomas Tuttill, and Mary Clarke," now turned to these additional accusations. It began by requiring Mary Clarke "to declare what Jonathan Coventry had done to her."

Clarke said that when Coventry came first to the town, he came to her master's to dwell there. On the second night, when her master and dame were in bed and she was getting ready to go to bed, John Knight came from Stratford and knocked at the door. She let him in. Her dame told her to give him his supper. As she was tending the fire, Coventry pulled her upon his knee, put her hand under her skirt, toward her naked belly, pulled out his member, and told her to take it in her hand. She refused. He forced her to touch it. She said she would tell her master, and he let her go. When he came to their house on another occasion, she went outside on some mission. (It was in the night.) He stood outside and attempted to hold and kiss her. Another time, as she was going along in the path, she saw him coming and went out of the way to avoid him. He came out of his way and met her. With his member in his hand, he touched against her belly in a filthy way.

Coventry denied these things, boldly alleging his innocence. If it were true, he would confess it, for "he that covers his sins shall not prosper, but whoso confesses and forsakes them shall have mercy" (Proverbs 28:13).

Thomas Tuttill was now called. Tuttill said that Coventry had told him, when they went in the woods together, that Clarke had a great tuft of hair betwixt her legs. Tuttill said, "How know you that?" Coventry replied that he had felt it and had handled her "member" and could see what was there. Tuttill saw Coventry and Clarke together that night. As Clarke said, Coventry kissed her. But Tuttill could not tell what they did. He saw Coventry go out of his way to meet Clarke and thrust himself against her belly with his member, as she said.

Coventry continued to deny the charge. Tuttill and Clarke then testified under oath that what they had charged him with was true. Coventry, "being fierce," said that if he had known their story to be true and had not confessed, but had instead gotten them to take an oath, he would have been guilty of taking God's name in vain, which would have been a high provocation. At this point, Coventry abruptly changed his story and confessed that all the witnesses had said was true. He was ashamed of it and under a great temptation when he so denied it. He desired the court to show favor to him.

Clarke further informed the court that one day, when she was coming to a shop, Tuttill was there and asked her if she had some hair betwixt her legs. She was ashamed. He told her to let him see, and he lifted up her skirt and looked.

Tuttill denied this. He said it is true he asked her such a question, thinking that Coventry had told a lie, but he did not lift up her skirt. But she herself lifted it up and said, "If you will not believe, you may see."

The court pronounced this behavior to be "abominably naughty filthy." It then proceeded to pronounce sentence.

Jonathan Coventry, for these filthy miscarriages, was ordered to be severely whipped.

Mary Clarke's former sentence of whipping was "further confirmed."

Tuttill received leniency. He showed himself most penitent for his fault. The principal part of his alleged miscarriage was testified to only by Clarke and denied by him, though he confessed he spoke very sinful words to her, of which he was ashamed. Considering the matter as it was presented, the court agreed to spare him from correction by whipping and ordered that he pay forty shillings as a fine to the jurisdiction.

On October 19, 1655, the court reconsidered the ten-pound fine it had previously imposed on William Judson. "Considering his age and weakness," the court decreased the fine by forty shillings.

As far as the records indicate, Knight was hanged, and Vincon, Clarke, and Coventry were whipped.

The Youth Sex Cases plainly suggest that the New Haven Colony's announced dedication to biblical principles was hardly sufficient to prevent sexual activity among the young. William Judson's farm seems to have been an epicenter of such activity.

Little of this activity seems to have been innocent, even by modern standards. John Knight sexually assaulted Peter Vincon and Mary Clarke. Jonathan Coventry sexually assaulted Clarke, apparently in Knight's presence. When Clarke wasn't being sexually assaulted in her workplace, Thomas Tuttill was sexually harassing her at the store. For Vincon and Clarke, Judson's farm was the workplace from hell.

These were young people. Vincon, we are told, was about fourteen years old, and Clarke must have been quite young as well, since it was considered remarkable that she had pubic hair.[4] The idea that these young people were whipped for the crime of being victims of a predatory sexual assault is appalling by any modern standard. It is doubtful that Clarke was comforted by the court's prayer that God would bless her stripes as she was being whipped.

Amidst these appalling punishments, however, one element of the Youth Sex Cases stands out as surprisingly modern. Apart from its views of sexual morality, the court saw these cases as raising a serious issue of workplace safety, at least with respect to child workers. It stated that the Judsons had a "trust and duty," both to Clarke and her parents, to protect her from abuse. For neglecting this trust, Judson was heavily fined, even though a portion of the fine was later remitted.

Two centuries later, children working in the Industrial Revolution's "dark satanic mills" would regularly be maimed and killed in unsafe industrial workplaces, and the courts would turn a deaf ear to their cries. This obliviousness was not restricted to Dickens's

England. In 1861, the Connecticut Supreme Court would say of a *ten-year-old boy* maimed while working in a cotton mill that the child-employee had assumed the risk of his employment and "must be held to have voluntarily taken upon himself this hazard when he entered into the defendants' service."[5] Regardless of its other faults, and they were many, the Court of Magistrates was not quite so oblivious in 1655. It saw employers as engaged in positions of trust.

18

❧

THE

DISPUTED

WILL

❧

On May 26, 1656, the Court of Magistrates gave routine approval to a number of wills made by recently deceased residents of the colony.[1] One testamentary matter, however, turned out to be far from routine. James Hindes, late of Southold,[2] had made a will, now presented to the court, giving his entire estate to his wife. The problem was that Hindes was also survived by minor children, and the widow was about to marry a man named Ralph Dayton.

Mr. Herbert of Southold, one of the overseers[3] appointed by Hindes's will, informed the court that, hearing of the widow's plans, he went to her and asked her to give something to the children before she married. The widow said, "No, not till she died." At last, however, she yielded to give the children twenty pounds apiece. But she would not confirm this until Dayton came. When Dayton arrived, he initially dissented and then "yielded to it." But when it came time to put the matter down in writing, the widow refused.

The court now turned to the widow. (We never learn her name.) When asked the reason for her refusal, she replied that her husband gave it to her, and she would keep it while she lived.

What would you say, the court asked, if your husband had given all away to the children and nothing to you? What would you have thought?[4] The court added that "men may not make wills as they will themselves but must attend the mind of God in doing the same, who doth provide that children (unless weighty reason be to the contrary) shall have portions, and the eldest a double portion.[5] Therefore, the rest must have a part. The Apostle saith, 'It is the duty of parents to lay up for their children.'[6] Therefore if they will consider and agree among themselves, it will well satisfy the Court, but if not, then the Court must issue it."

After some debate among themselves, Dayton and the widow asked the court to decide the case. But Dayton also informed the court that a cow and a calf had been lost since the goods were appraised, as well as three or four goats. Dayton also said that the house and the land were appraised "very much too dear." He further said that Hindes's eldest son had already had his father's tools given him.

The court took all of this into account. It ordered that the loss of the cow, calf, and goats be borne by the widow and her children, as well as "what loss shall appear to be in the house and land." The tools would be reckoned as part of the estate. The estate, as recalculated, would be equally divided, half to the widow and half to the children, with the eldest having a double portion. If the children were, with the consent of the overseers, "put out to trade," their charges would come out of their own portions. A bond previously placed on Dayton to ensure his appearance in court would remain until these obligations had been fulfilled.

Dayton told the court that "what was done in the case betwixt his wife and children doth well satisfy them." He added that, before James Hindes died, he desired Mr. Herbert to be replaced as an overseer by William Wells. The court responded that it could do nothing without proof, but if proved "that it was the man's mind before he died," two of the court's deputies would join the other overseer "to take care of the children and their estates, that they may be put out to trades and their estates improved to their advantage."

※※※

The Disputed Will Case was not decided in a legal vacuum. In 1655, the General Court had asked the governor to compile a book of laws for the colony to be printed in England.[7] The printed volumes[8] did not arrive in New Haven until after the Disputed Will Case had been decided, but the court had approved the manuscript prior to its shipment to London and would have been familiar with its contents. The resulting volume contained two provisions pertinent to this case. One provision, governing the law of dower, gave a surviving wife the right to a one-third life interest in her deceased husband's property. A second provision, governing the law of wills, stated that if the decedent was survived by children "not duly provided for," they were to receive "two third parts at most . . . with . . . the eldest son . . . to have a double child's portion."

Under this law, Hindes's widow was statutorily entitled to a one-third life interest in his estate. The court had discretion to order that Hindes's children receive part, or even all, of the remaining two-thirds. In giving half of Hindes's estate to his widow and half to his children, the court acted well within its legal discretion.

The substantive merits of its decision aside, the court's procedural approach to the Disputed Will Case was exemplary. Although the court could simply have imposed its will by judicial fiat (something we have seen on more than one occasion), it did not do so here. Rather, it reasoned with the litigants and urged them to consult with each other in the process. It explained the biblical law governing the case. It asked Hindes's widow a telling question based on the Golden Rule: if this had been done to you, wouldn't *you* want the court to step in? It issued a decision on the merits only after the parties had jointly asked it to do so.

As modern judges know all too well, family disputes can easily lead to endless bitterness and strife. Will contests are often seen as zero-sum games, where one litigant's gain can only be obtained by an opposing litigant's loss. The Court of Magistrates managed to avoid this scenario, not only by reasoning with the litigants but also by urging them to consult with each other about the process. In doing so, it acted commendably.

19

❧

THE FARMHAND

ARSONIST

❧

On May 28, 1656, the General Court called the case of John Frost, a fourteen-year-old servant to William Gibbard, a former deputy of the court.[1] The governor had previously examined Frost on March 17, and Frost now repeated a confession he had made to the governor on that occasion about a fire he had set the previous day. This is what he told the court.

March 16, 1656, was a Sunday. That afternoon, while Gibbard and his wife were at the meetinghouse, Frost lit a piece of paper at the fire in the house and carried it out under his hat, so that the children would not see it. He went to a haystack near the barn and on purpose kindled some hay, with the intent to burn both hay and barn. He left the hay smoking and went to the meetinghouse without any endeavor to put it out. As he desired, the fire burned the hay and barn. Unfortunately, the fire ran to the Gibbards' dwelling house and burned that to the ground as well, along with many goods. When Frost saw what had happened, he repented and was sorry for what he had done.

The court asked Frost what had stirred him up to do this and how long these purposes had been in his mind.

Frost replied that he didn't like to plow with his master because when the oxen didn't behave, his master would hit him. Therefore he had a mind to burn the hay. He also did it for revenge because, about six weeks before this, his master had whipped him. From that time, he had plans to do this thing. He had further been stirred up to do this about a fortnight later, when his master struck him a blow. He would have done it sooner if he could have had the opportunity to do it so that nobody would see him. He had also been hindered by rain and snow. He sometimes thought to do it in the night, but he thought that might hurt their persons.

Gibbard told the court that it was likely he had sometimes struck Frost for miscarriages; he thought boys sometimes deserve this punishment. Gibbard had also whipped him, as Frost had told the court. The whipping was for lying, and Gibbard thought it was his duty to correct him for this. He thought that one time he struck Frost a blow because he left the barn door open and some calves had gone in and eaten pease. But he thought that if the court considered what the boy was when Gibbard took him in and how he was now, it would appear that he had been well treated and had not had any immoderate correction. Of late, Frost had behaved so pleasantly in the family that it was a marvel to see, particularly the day before he did this mischief and even that morning. He should wonder at this, but he knew that Frost had behaved very hypocritically on other occasions.

When asked to respond, Frost said he had behaved as he did so that he might not be suspected for the mischief he intended to do.

Given Frost's full and free confession, the court seriously considered what God called for in this case. Considering Frost's young age and the fact that he was "somewhat childish in his way," the court agreed to spare his life, notwithstanding the fact that the offense was exceedingly heinous and aggravated with many circumstances. It instead imposed the following sentence. Frost was sentenced to be a servant for twenty-one years. Five or six of these years belonged to Gibbard, being the remainder of the time due to him by a former agreement. For the remaining fifteen or sixteen years, more or less, the profits of Frost's servitude would be divided between Gibbard and John Wakeman, a deputy of the court,[2] who had, we are told, sustained an economic loss in the fire. This division would be made in a due proportion when the several losses were made known.

The court was not done. Frost was to be "severely whipped with rods fit for that purpose." He was also to "wear a halter about his neck and a small light lock upon his leg," so that these marks of shame would be seen. He was to stand in the "pillory" (stocks) for as long as the magistrates saw fit. If he were to go out of the jurisdiction without leave, he would be liable to forfeit his life. This sentence would be published and executed on the next training day, June 9. The charges for his imprisonment[3] would be paid by the jurisdiction rather than by his master, who had lost so much already.

Gibbard was troubled by the sentence. He told the court that some of his neighbors were not willing to have the boy dwell with him again, fearing he would do more mischief of a similar kind. He additionally objected to Frost's wearing of the lock because it would be a hindrance to him in his work and so make his service less profitable.

The court told Gibbard that it could not force any man to take Frost, but if Gibbard could not himself employ Frost to his satisfaction, he could negotiate with someone else to take him. The court suggested its own member, Deputy Wakeman; the court's marshal; and John Cooper, who owned an iron works, as possibilities. If Gibbard could agree with any of these, the court would be content. But if no one would take him, Frost would have to be sent away, perhaps back to England to his father. In that case, the court would have to meet "to consider of some further punishment to be inflicted for example and terror to others, that none may be emboldened to take such courses." If the lock proved inconvenient and a hindrance in Frost's labor, the court could alter that condition as it saw fit.

This was not the last that we (or the court) will hear of Frost. He will appear in 1662 as the Lecherous Swineherd. But that will be another story.

❦

Given the law of the era, Frost was fortunate that he wasn't hanged.[4] But any praise of the court's actual sentence—a sentence given after due consideration of God's perceived will—must be muted indeed. The underlying facts of the case are unrelentingly grim. Frost was a fourteen-year-old boy who was, we are told, "somewhat childish in his way." His father was in England, and we are told nothing of his mother. He was bound as an indentured servant in a strange land to a master who beat and whipped him as he would a farm animal. Gibbard seems to have been an American version of Wackford Squeers, the brutish boarding school proprietor immortalized by Charles Dickens in *Nicholas Nickleby*.

Frost does not appear to have been entirely malevolent. It seems reasonably clear that he did not intend to burn his master's house or to harm any member of the family. The only justification for the numerous physical punishments ordered to be inflicted on him—whipping with rods, a halter around the neck, a lock upon his leg, and standing in the pillory—was, in the court's words, to be an "example and terror to others, that none may be emboldened to take such courses." In pronouncing this punishment, the court emulated Frost's brutal master, who had already beaten and whipped his youthful servant, reaping a harvest of anger and destruction. By combining these exemplary punishments with twenty-one years of judicially imposed servitude—much of it for the economic benefit of a member of the court—the court acted in a way that could hardly be justified by any modern standard.

20

‹‹‹‹‹‹

THE STOLEN

SILVERWARE

‹‹‹‹‹‹

George Wood, a servant of Stephen Goodyear, the deputy governor of the colony and a sitting member of the Court of Magistrates, was a chronic thief.[1] The difficulty in the case wasn't proof
of his guilt. That was established by overwhelming evidence. The
problem was what to do with him following his conviction at a
time when the option of long-term incarceration did not exist.

Wood was called before the Court of Magistrates on September
5, 1656.[2] This was not his first appearance before the court. He
had been brought before it "about a year" previously "for sundry
miscarriages." One of those "miscarriages" had been the theft of two
silver spoons from Samuel Eaton, himself a sitting magistrate at
the time.[3] The missing spoons had never been found. The court had
threatened to expel Wood from the colony, but security had been
given for his good behavior, and he was now working for Goodyear.

A week before Wood's second appearance, on the Sabbath, a
"great disturbance" had occurred in the Goodyear family. A knife
was missing. Some members of the family accused Wood of stealing it. Wood denied the charge and said that if they would not believe him, they could search his chest. Goodyear's daughter, Hope

Lamberton, went upstairs with him. Wood opened his chest and made a show of displaying its contents, tumbling things up and down. But, "by providence," Lamberton saw the haft (handle) of the knife, since it was brass and very discernable, and came down and told her mother.

Wood again denied the charge and, bitterly cursing himself, wished that the knife was in his heart's blood if he had it. At that, Goodyear, being much troubled, told Wood that it was necessary that the thing should be cleared and that some other person should go to see.

Mrs. Goodyear went upstairs with Wood. Now, however, Wood refused to open his chest, saying that the people below would laugh at him. Mr. Goodyear then went up himself. When he arrived, Wood had thrown the knife out of the window. He told Goodyear to look in the chest to see if any knife was there.

Hope said that Wood had "an Indian bag" that had some things in it. Mrs. Goodyear searched Wood's bed and found the bag wrapped up in a waistcoat inside a pillow. Wood snatched the bag out of Mrs. Goodyear's hands. Mr. Goodyear caught hold of it, and the two of them pulled at it to get possession. Wood, seeing that he couldn't pull the bag out of Goodyear's hands, pulled it before him. He fell down, laid on it, and put it in his breeches. He then rose up and tried to run away. Goodyear held on to Wood. Somehow, Wood got into another room where a heap of pease lay on the floor. He pulled something out of his breeches and threw it in the pease. Someone saw him do this. When they looked, they discovered two silver spoons. When Wood saw that the spoons had been discovered, his countenance fell. Being asked whose they were, he said they were Mr. Samuel Eaton's. These were the spoons he had been accused of stealing the previous year. The marks on the spoons, including the gold-smith's marks, had been filed off.

Wood was brought before the governor that evening. He was informed that, considering his former and present miscarriages, he must be committed to prison. Wood begged not to go. His entreaties not prevailing, he threatened to kill himself or to kill or be killed. Since he refused to go, the governor was forced to send his own servants to assist the marshal and cause irons to be put on the prisoner. In spite of all this, Wood broke out of the prison that night. Had a watch not been set on purpose, he might have escaped.

When Wood was brought before the court, his attitude changed. He wished to speak for himself. He seemed sorrowful and confessed that all the charges against him were true. His miscarriages had been very great. He blessed God, who had dis-covered him and afflicted him, for by this he more clearly saw his condition and hoped it would be a warning to him.

The court was unconvinced of Wood's repentance. After con-sidering his miscarriages, it sentenced him to be set in the pillory for an hour with a paper fixed to the pillory by him declaring his miscarriages. After that, Wood was to be severely whipped, so he and others would learn to fear such courses. Wood had previously been expelled from the plantation for his miscarriages and had been saved only by security given for his good behavior. He had now fallen again into these and worse behaviors, namely, steal-ing, lying, cursing himself, threatening to kill himself or others, mocking his mistress, rebelling against his master and against the authority in this place—and this on the Sabbath Day—and filing off the marks of the spoons stolen, "one of which would have been death in some other place."[4]

For these reasons, the court judged Wood "not fit to live among them." He was now banished out of the jurisdiction. If he were found in the jurisdiction again, death would be executed upon him without any further sentencing proceeding. Because, however, Mr. Goodyear had lain out some money for him and it was fit that Goodyear should be repaid,[5] the court gave Goodyear fourteen days to sell Wood's services[6] in any of the other colonies or take some other course to recover his security. Until then, Wood was to lie in prison in irons to prevent any more miscarriages.

⬥⬥⬥⬥⬥

By modern standards, the penalty visited on Wood—the pillory, followed by whipping and banishment—was remarkably severe for the theft of a knife and two spoons. The Supreme Court has declared banishment "a fate universally decried by civilized people" and would doubtless look the same way at the pillory and the lash.[7] But the court was undoubtedly correct when it observed that Wood would have been hanged in England for the same offense. By that contemporary standard, at least, the court was merciful by allowing Wood to live.

The New Haven Colony, however, professed to be governed by biblical standards and, as we have seen, was particularly influenced by the dictates of the Old Testament, especially in criminal cases. Although biblical law could be oppressively harsh in many cases, its punishment for theft was surprisingly lenient. Under the law of Exodus, if an animal is stolen, the thief must "make restitution unto to the owner thereof" (Exodus 22:12).[8] The 1656 New Haven Colony laws ostensibly followed this precept in requiring restitution for theft as well. The laws added, however, that "if the thief in any part of the premises be not able to make restitution (if the case require it) he is to be sold for a servant, till by his labor he may make due restitution."[9] This presumably provided the court with the authority for allowing Goodyear to sell Wood's services. The additional sentences of the pillory and the lash were, however, added by the court without either biblical or statutory authority.

21

∞∞∞

THE VANISHED

HUSBAND

∞∞∞

Lovers lost beyond the sea may be a staple of English folk songs, but real instances of persons vanished without a trace must have occurred from time to time in the age of sail.[1] On March 25, 1657,[2] a case involving such a disappearance came before the Court of Magistrates.

John Tompson appeared before the court claiming the property[3] of John Roberts, now in the hands of John Wakeman, the treasurer of the New Haven Colony. He also claimed Roberts's property in Saybrook held by John Westall and some additional property owned by Roberts in Rhode Island.

Tompson claimed Roberts's property on behalf of Tompson's present wife, the former Ann Vicars. Almost four years previously, Vicars had married Roberts. Roberts had subsequently traveled to England, promising to return. Before Roberts left, Tompson said, he had given everything that he had in this country to Vicars. Contrary to his promise, Roberts had not returned. Tompson and his wife had heard nothing of his whereabouts. According to Tompson, Roberts's property was owed to his wife when she demanded it, and she was now making that demand.

The court responded cautiously. "What is in other places, this court meddles not, but with that which is in this jurisdiction." Because this case concerned an absent man, it had to be especially wary "and act upon clear proof." If Tompson had witnesses, he should produce them.

Tompson produced a written statement by John Thomas dated January 5, 1657.[4] According to Thomas, Roberts had told him in Milford "that whether he lived or died, he gave all his estate that he had in New Haven and at Rhode Island (in case he came no more) to his contracted wife."

Thomas Harrison, who was in court, testified under oath that he had heard Roberts say when he went away "that he had given to Ann Vicars his whole estate in New England, whether he lived or died."

Anthony Elcott testified that he had heard Roberts say, both at waterside and aboard the vessel on which he went away, that "if he proved inconstant," whether he lived or died, he gave what he had here to Vicars. Roberts further said that Vicars could go to Wakeman, whom he had entrusted with his estate, and take what she would.

Having heard the evidence, the court explained that it was unclear exactly when Roberts's gift of his property to his wife was to have become effective. Three possible alternatives were presented by the evidence: (1) the gift might have become effective if Roberts "proved inconstant"; (2) the gift might have been triggered by Roberts's death; or (3) according to Thomas's testimony, the gift might have become effective upon Roberts's failure to return. The evidence, however, left the court uncertain as to which condition Roberts had actually intended.

There was, the court said, another problem as well. Once the intended event had occurred, exactly what property was Vicars to receive? Was she to receive Roberts's entire estate? Alternatively, should she simply receive "something for her present use"? The court could not "judge it rational" that Roberts "should give away his estate in such a manner from himself."

Finally, the court said, it was questionable whether the claimed property had really belonged to Roberts in the first place. It was possible that the property in fact belonged to Roberts's mother.

Given these concerns, the court denied Tompson's claim until "more full light appear."

⋆⋇⋆⋇⋆

The court was surely correct in treating Tompson's claim cautiously. Roberts had married Vicars less than four years previously, and the period of his disappearance had been even shorter. His return was hardly inconceivable, and if he returned to find Tompson in control of his property, the complications would be embarrassing for the court and difficult to unravel.

The now-familiar common-law rule that a person who has not been heard of for seven years is presumed dead did not yet exist.[5] The prior rule had been that a missing person was presumed to be living until the contrary was proved.[6] Under either rule, Roberts could hardly have been found dead. He had not been missing for seven years, and there was no proof of his demise.

But given its predilection for finding sexual peccadillos in other cases, the court was remarkably incurious about the status of Vicars. How had a woman who had married Roberts less than four years previously now become married to Tompson?[7] When it came to Roberts's property, the court was more than willing to wait to see if Roberts would still turn up. If he did turn up, he would surely be no happier to see his wife than his property in the arms of Tompson. Perhaps there had been a divorce, unmentioned in the records. Regardless of the situation, the court was simply unwilling to disturb the status quo, whatever it may have been, in the absence of further evidence.

22

❀❀

THE

ATTEMPTED

BESTIALITY

CASE

❀❀

In 1657, the Court of Magistrates convicted John Ferris of the crime of attempted bestiality.[1] The case was omitted, for reasons of propriety, from the printed New Haven Colony records by the 1858 publisher. The record of the trial survives in the original manuscript in the Connecticut State Archives, and it is from that manuscript that the following account is taken.

On July 30, 1657,[2] Ferris was called before the court and "charged with the sin of bestiality." The proof began with "a testimony of Henry Accerly, taken upon oath, affirmed to the same before John Ferris."[3]

Accerly testified that one night about sunset, he had seen Ferris stand on a log behind a cow. Ferris had the cow's tail in one hand and "his privy member" in the other. Accerly saw Ferris draw himself back and "draw forth his member out of the cow's body."

Accerly was in a "maze" at this time (perhaps a corn maze). He called to Ferris and asked what he was doing. Ferris stepped off the log and said that he was "milking." Accerly responded that if it wasn't milking, it would bring him to the gallows.

Accerly testified that he was quite near Ferris on one side of him, so he could plainly see what had happened, even though it was almost night and rainy weather. He then went to Angel Hubbard and told him what he had seen. They both went to Ferris and confronted him with Accerly's observations. Ferris initially denied the accusation but afterward partly confessed. "He was doing of it but had not done the act." Hubbard then gave his own testimony of the events that night.

Ferris was called upon to speak. Ferris said he was out in the field about sunset, milking the cow. He was lifting the tail off her back when he had to urinate. He drew forth his member, and an evil thought ran through his mind. He stepped upon the log and attempted it, but considering what an odious thing it was, he withdrew before Accerly called to him.

Accerly repeated to the court that, in his examination taken at Stamford, he had said Ferris had initially denied he had ever done any such thing but had subsequently confessed that he did attempt the thing and draw forth his member to do it, but did not follow through.

The court considered the matter as it had been presented and "advised with the elders and received their judgment in this case." It declared that Ferris had committed "a most abominable sin." One witness had proved it to be "the full act of bestiality." "Were there another witness or other evidence to confirm it," the punishment "could be no less than death." Ferris's own confession is that he attempted it and drew out his member to that purpose. Though he had said that his own conscience had condemned the sin as odious and had caused him to withdraw, the court did not believe it. Instead the court believed he had either done the act or would have proceeded further if the discovery had not prevented it.

But taking the evidence "in the most sparing way according to his own confession," the court decided on a sentence that would be "an example of terror to others." Ferris would first be "severely whipped" in New Haven. Afterward, "as soon as he may be fit," he would again be whipped in like matter at Stamford. A halter would be put around his neck, and he must always *wear* this halter visibly, until the court saw cause to alter it. Ferris was ordered to pay a fine of twenty pounds to the jurisdiction for the charge and trouble to which he had put it. He was additionally ordered to pay all charges to the marshal and to Accerly, so they would not suffer loss from such a lewd person. Finally, until Ferris had received his "second correction" at Stamford, he would remain in safe custody as a prisoner in Stamford.

⚜

Although the facts of the Attempted Bestiality Case might have offended nineteenth-century sensibilities, the printers of that era did a disservice to later readers by omitting it from publication, since the case turns out to be one of exceptional interest. Two features stand out. First, the court's finding that, although Ferris had not actually *committed* the crime with which he had been charged, he was nevertheless guilty of an *attempt* to commit that crime was something of a pioneering decision in the law of attempted crimes. Second, harsh though Ferris's punishment was, the fact that the defendant was allowed to live indicates that the court was, at long last, beginning to show some minimal mercy in sex cases.

The doctrine that the law should punish a defendant who attempts to commit a crime but is, for reasons other than his own change of mind, unable to complete it is universally accepted today. If I intend to kill you with a gun and shoot at you, only to have the gun misfire, I'm not guilty of murder, because you're still alive, but I'm still guilty of attempted murder. If I go into a bank intending to rob it and am stopped by a security officer at the door before I complete an actual robbery, I'm still guilty of attempted robbery. To most people, this is just common sense. The idea is to subject dangerous people to corrective action before it's too late. If the law lets me go free after I shoot at you because my gun has misfired, it's only a matter of time before I get my act together and successfully complete my intended crime.

This was not always the case. The early common law proceeded on the principle that an attempt to do harm is no offense.[4] Early in the seventeenth century, the infamous English Court of Star Chamber occasionally punished criminal attempts, but that court went out of business in 1640.[5] The modern law of criminal attempts is a product of the late eighteenth century.[6] Seen in this light, the Court of Magistrates anticipated the development of modern law by more than a century.

But while the modern law of attempt was developed to *expand* criminal liability, the motive of the Court of Magistrates was quite different. The court developed the law in the way it did as a means of showing *mercy* to the offender. "Mercy," of course, is a relative term. Ferris was whipped, haltered, fined, and imprisoned, but he was nevertheless allowed to live, while earlier in the colony's history, he would have been sent straight to the gallows. The court conspicuously stretched to reach this result, for if we take it at its word, it did not even believe Ferris's version of events. In any case, it appears that some cracks in the previously unbending biblical law governing the colony were beginning to appear. Whatever Ferris had done, the court was unwilling to send him to the gallows. In at least this limited sense, it was tempering justice with mercy.

23

❦

THE CLAMOROUS

QUAKER

❦

In the trial of Richard Crabb "for several miscarriages," the leaders of the New Haven Colony reached new levels of religious intolerance.[1]

On May 31, 1658, Crabb, being bound over from his home in Greenwich, appeared before the Court of Magistrates. Crabb's wife (her first name is never mentioned) had also been ordered to appear, but Crabb told the court she was unable to come. The court declared that Crabb "was now called to answer for several miscarriages by many clamorous and reproachful speeches against the ministry, government, and officers [and] neglecting of meetings for sanctification of the Sabbath."

The court first read the testimony of William Oliver, who had testified under oath on December 1, 1657. Oliver testified that he had come to Crabb's house "with the rest" to "demand the Quaker's books." Goodwife Crabb went into another room and shut the door. When Crabb opened the door, Goodwife Crabb emerged to denounce the intruders, saying to them, "Is this your fasting and praying, to come and rob us and rob men's houses?" She held up her hands and said, "The vengeance of God hangs over your head at Stamford for taking away our land without commission." She then railed at the ministers and said they were Baal's priests, preaching for hire. She would not hear them. The intruders were shedders of "the blood of the saints of God."

One of Oliver's companions was Francis Bell, a deputy for Stamford. Goodwife Crabb called him a traitor, a liar, and a villain and said his posterity would suffer for his iniquity. Bell denied this and said he hoped Goodwife Crabb was not a witch. She replied that Bell was a rogue or a rascal.

Goodwife Crabb then turned to John Waterbury, another deputy for Stamford who had joined Oliver's company. She called Waterbury a traitor. Oliver recounted that she subsequently assailed other members of the company with bitter words.

Jonathan Renalls had testified under oath on May 13, 1658. According to Renalls, Goodwife Crabb had given "very bad language" to Bell. Bell responded, "Woman, I thought your religion had been thee and thou." Goodwife Crabb replied that her religion "is as good as yours."

The final testimony read to the court was that of George Slawson, given under oath on May 24, 1658. Slawson testified that he had gone to Greenwich with Daniel Scofield, the marshal, to apprehend one Thomas Marshall. They came to Crabb's house and seized Marshall there. Crabb asked to see the warrant. When he saw it, he questioned its extent. Crabb asked the marshal to stay until morning and offered security. Slawson refused.

Goodwife Crabb began to rail at Slawson's company, saying they had "stolen away Greenwich." Slawson responded, "Goodwife Crabb, I should be glad to see you at Stamford meeting." She replied that she would never come while she lived, adding, "What shall I come to hear, to cast away my soul to the devil?"

Crabb not only failed to rebuke his wife but also had the temerity to "countenance" her and Marshall and question what ground Slawson's company had to do as it did.

Governor Francis Newman, who presided over the court, told Crabb that the testimony heard by the court established "notorious things" that "must not be suffered." Crabb agreed but said that "he could not reclaim her."

Francis Bell affirmed that Crabb had "seemed to countenance her in it," although Goodwife Crabb had continued her railing speeches for almost an hour. When she had called for drink to refresh her, Crabb had given her such drink, which strengthened her "to go on in those wicked speeches, which was dreadful to hear." She had lifted up her hands toward heaven and said, "Holy Father, power out thy vengeance upon them." Finally, when she began to speak out against authority, Crabb quieted her, telling her that she would hurt herself. In addition, Crabb had himself vilified the ordinances and ministers.

The court told Crabb that he had been a "harborer of Quakers" and had kept Quakers' books in his house. Crabb replied that indeed Marshall had been there, but he did not account Marshall to be a Quaker "nor anything else than a weathercock."

The governor demanded that Crabb tell the court whether he considered the Lord's Day to be the Christian Sabbath, sanctified by virtue of the fourth commandment. Crabb answered in the affirmative. The court responded that he had previously "held out the contrary." Crabb replied, "It was one thing to speak in way of discourse and another to speak positively."

Richard Law, another deputy for Stamford, testified that he and Francis Bell had spoken with Crabb, and he had propounded such questions concerning the Sabbath that they concluded his judgment "was against the morality of it."

The court asked Crabb if he would give security for his future "quiet and Christian carriage." In addition, would he show ministers that respect that was due to them? Crabb responded that he did not feel safe in doing so, having so many eyes upon him, but he resolved to walk inoffensively while he remained in Greenwich and to eventually remove himself from the town. The court opined that "a remove was easier to him than a reformation," but he must expect that Greenwich would be no place for him unless he reformed. The court looked on Crabb's miscarriages as very great and said it would declare his sentence the next morning.

The next day, June 1, 1658, the court called Crabb before it. The governor told him that he had read again the written evidence of "notorious miscarriages" submitted to the court the previous day. Crabb answered that, notwithstanding these writings, he knew his own sincerity and believed that God would not impute those things to him. He added, "If this be religion, it is strange religion."

The governor responded with a story he had heard about Crabb. Crabb had met two men from the Massachusetts Bay Colony and asked them from whence they came. When they said they came from Concord, Crabb responded that it was "a beggarly place." When they replied that it was a good place, Crabb said that the priest and the people who had come thence were almost starved. When the men answered that they had no priest, Crabb replied, "I see you are in darkness, as all the country is."

The governor followed this up with a second story imputed to Crabb. Crabb had asked a woman in Norwalk "when she would be perfect." When she answered that this would happen when she came to heaven, Crabb told her that she might be perfect here.

In making these statements, the court told Crabb, he had spoken like a Quaker. He comported himself as if he would take all opportunities to corrupt others with whom he conversed. Crabb responded that these statements had been made "only by way of discourse."

The governor announced that if anyone had something to say in the case, he might now speak. Bell responded by saying that the particular wrong done to him should be considered. Having been sent by authority, he had been called a traitor, a liar, a villain, and a rascal. If he was guilty of these things, he was worthy to die.

When Crabb denied that he had spoken these words, he was told that if his wife had spoken these words and he had countenanced her, he must answer for them.

The court asked Bell if he had spoken expecting justice for himself or as a witness to a crime committed by an evildoer. Bell replied that he never had an action against any man and would be content in this case if the court saw and acknowledged "evil in these miscarriages." He further declared that it was the desire of the freemen that the court would take some course to ensure that their peace was preserved, their ordinances promoted, and their minister encouraged by suppressing those whose actions and speeches tended to be contrary. "If Quakers may be entertained, their books laid open and read and questions raised concerning the truths of God—What do you think of this, and what do you say to that?"—who knows "what ill things will come in a short time?"

John Bishop, the pastor of the church at Stamford, told the court that there was a "leaven"[2] spread among the young people of Stamford concerning the Sabbath and the written word of God. Turning to Crabb, Bishop said, "How far you are guilty, you have cause to consider, but you must know you have given occasion of suspicion that it proceeds from you. There is a maid detained by you, to the grief of her parents, who is corrupted." Bishop concluded that Crabb could not continue at Stamford unless some course were taken to remove and reform these grievances.

Crabb asked to speak concerning his wife, not to justify her in any evil but to acquaint the court with some things concerning her. She had been well bred in England and was a zealous professor of religion from her childhood, almost beyond example, but when she was suddenly surprised, she had not the power to restrain her passions.

The governor replied that what Crabb had said greatly aggravated his wife's miscarriages, for "if she had been a great professor, it was certain she had been an ill practitioner." Crabb had countenanced and supported her, which suggested that he had fallen into evils of the like nature. Mr. Bishop had been reviled as a priest of Baal and the members of his church as liars. It had been further said that Bishop preached for filthy lucre.

The court called on Crabb to consider his way, how after a great profession made, he had now been for a long time a neglector of the ordinances and a reproacher of the ministry. His wife was also these things, and he had not reproved her. Their case seemed scarcely to be paralleled in these times. "Having had such light," along with his wife, he had fallen into abominable courses and railed upon ministers, calling them Baal's priests and calling the people of God traitors, liars, and villains. Every ordinary eye might see marks of apostasy on him. Crabb was called to consider this seriously.

Bell told Crabb he had formerly had a good esteem of him, but now he feared Crabb's parts were turned against the churches of Christ.

Crabb told the court he had nothing more to say but that the Lord would help him.

The court considered these miscarriages, which it looked upon as very grievous and of a high nature. Crabb was ordered to pay a fine to the jurisdiction of thirty pounds and to post a one-hundred-pound standing security for his good behavior. He was further ordered to make a public acknowledgment at Stamford, to the satisfaction of Bell and others that he had wronged. If he did not do so, he was ordered to pay an additional fine.

❧❧❧❧❧

Woe betide the religious dissenter in the New Haven Colony. The colony's leaders committed the real crimes in this case. The actual hero of the story is Crabb's unnamed wife, who had the fortitude to denounce political authorities entering a private home in order to "demand the Quaker's books." From a modern perspective, the idea of government officials entering a private home without a warrant to search private books and papers is deeply troubling. The Fourth Amendment, adopted in 1791, specifically recognizes "the right of the people to be secure in their persons, houses, papers, and effects, against unreasonable searches and seizures." This provision of our Bill of Rights was inspired by a famous English case,[3] decided in 1765, in which the lord chief justice of England awarded substantial damages to a British political dissident whose home had been searched by authorities looking for allegedly seditious newspapers. "By the laws of England," the chief justice declared, "every invasion of private property, be it ever so minute, is a trespass."[4] Crabb's wife could not have agreed more.

The New Haven of 1658, however, was a different world. Dissenting religious thoughts were punished, and the homes of suspected dissenters were not secure. Husbands who did not control their wives' expressions were held liable for their utterances. It comes as no surprise that Crabb wished to remove himself from the colony. For those with dissenting viewpoints, life in the colony must have been intolerable.

24

๑๑๑๑

THE CURRIER'S
APPRENTICE

๑๑๑๑

Later on the same day in 1658 that it heard the Clamorous Quaker, the Court of Magistrates heard a complicated case involving a contract between a currier and his apprentice.[1]

The currier was one John Meigs, almost certainly same the New Haven leather and shoe merchant that we met as "John Meges" in 1647 in the Faulty Shoes. Meigs (we'll use the 1658 spelling of his name here) had taken on as an apprentice an orphan named Thomas Wheadon.[2] The contract with Wheadon was supposed to last seven years, but shortly after the contract had been signed, Meigs had transferred Wheadon's servitude to one Matthew Gilbert, a magistrate who, as it happened, was a member of the very Court of Magistrates hearing the case. Wheadon now declared to the court that "he had received wrong from Goodman Meigs." In modern legal terms, Wheadon was suing Meigs for breach of contract.

To make his case, Wheadon presented the court with an "indenture." An "indenture," as readers of *Oliver Twist* will recall, was a contract by which an apprentice was bound to a master who would undertake to teach him a trade.[3] After Wheadon had read the indenture to the court, Meigs asked what he had done wrong. What part of the covenant was not performed. Wheadon answered that he had not been taught the trade of a currier.

One William Potter declared to the court that Wheadon had been done a great wrong because he had not been taught his promised trade.

Governor Francis Newman, who presided over the court, demanded of Meigs why Wheadon had not been taught his trade according to the covenant. Meigs gave a lengthy explanation in response. The contract with Wheadon had been signed aboard a ship sailing from England to New England. Wheadon was to serve him for seven years from the time he came ashore. While they were in the ship, Meigs voluntarily engaged to teach Wheadon his trade. But when they arrived in New England, Gilbert "desired one of his servants." Meigs decided that, if Wheadon were willing, Gilbert should have him for five years. Wheadon consented to the arrangement. Meigs emphasized that both Wheadon's initial decision to learn the trade and his subsequent decision to transfer his servitude to Gilbert for five years had been voluntary on his part.

Meigs then presented the court with a second indenture that said Wheadon was previously bound to a master in England. According to Meigs, the English master had assigned to him this second indenture.

Wheadon denied this allegation and said a fellow passenger, Joseph Rabbins, could corroborate his own version of events. Wheadon said he had kept the English indenture on his person while aboard the ship. While he was asleep, however, the master of the ship took the indenture out of his pocket. The master kept the indenture for two or three days and, after calling him into his cabin, read it in his presence.

The court told Meigs that, if Wheadon's story was true (a proposition that Meigs denied), "it was irrational that he should have an indenture from [Wheadon's] master in England without an assignment."

Responding to this question, Meigs waffled. He had initially been "positive" that he had the rights of Wheadon's English master. But, given the court's question, he realized his confidence had been "too much." He now "only conceived" that he had these rights.

At this point, Wheadon produced the written testimony of Rabbins. Rabbins testified that Meigs had bound Wheadon to his apprenticeship when Wheadon was at sea, away from his friends. Meigs promised to teach him the trade of a currier, or cause him to be so taught, "so that he might be a perfect workman in his trade." Wheadon, however, was not willing to bind himself to an indenture for longer than five years. Wheadon had asked, weeping, "Why should I be bound for seven years and Joe Rabbins but for four?" Wheadon's master answered him hastily, "Thou fool you, thou wilt have a better trade than Joe Rabbins. Thou must get ten shillings in a day."

Having read Rabbins's testimony, the court told Meigs that "this had a show of circumvention" of Wheadon's rights. It demanded that Meigs tell it why Wheadon had been bound three years longer than Rabbins.

Meigs replied that Rabbins's circumstances were different. Rabbins already had a trade. In any event, Wheadon had voluntarily engaged to Gilbert, and if there was any question about earning capacity, he himself had curried three hides in a day.[4]

One Christopher Todd affirmed to the court that a currier could earn ten shillings a day. But the court replied that "this looked too like flapp."[5] It added that it had witnessed such "offensive passages" in Meigs before.

Meigs now turned to a clever legal argument. If he had apprenticed Wheadon to Gilbert for seven years with his consent, "he had done him no wrong." The implication was that Wheadon could not have been harmed by a briefer servitude.

The governor replied that "Wheadon was not of a capacity to dispose of himself." Meigs, the governor said, should not have supplied Wheadon's engagement to Gilbert by making a new agreement, even though "by arguments" he gained his consent.

Meigs now tried a new tack. After Wheadon's five-year servitude with Gilbert had ended, there would still remain two years in which Meigs could teach him the trade. In fact, Meigs asserted, he could teach a man "the essence of currying" in two *months.*

The court was not persuaded. It told Meigs that it was known that "there is so much mystery in the trade" that some persons, following a longer apprenticeship than two years, had still been found altogether insufficient. A letter from one Richard Church of Hartford asserted that Wheadon had been wronged by being withheld so long from the trade.

Meigs claimed that one "Murwin of Milford" would undertake to teach Wheadon his trade within two years, but the court pointed out that Murwin was a tanner rather than a currier[6] and thus had an entirely different trade.

Edward Church declared that his father had a man in England prepare for the trade for four years, and the man was still insufficient for the trade, although he had constant employment.

Meigs offered to train Wheadon for two years, and if that was insufficient, he would answer for any damages. The court answered that it "must not run so great a hazard."

Meigs tried again. There was, he said, a mistake in the date of the indenture that should be rectified.

The court responded that, if there was a mistake, it could be considered, but it needed to attend to "the business itself." Although Meigs had presented a document referring to a master in England, it did not appear that Meigs had any right to Wheadon, from either the English master or Wheadon's parents. Wheadon, rather, was a free man. He had been placed with his English master by virtue of legal authority. To alter his status, especially by transplanting him from England to New Haven, required similar authority. No such legal authority appeared here. There was only an agreement with an orphan, without consent of either master or magistrate. That agreement, moreover, was obtained by the misleading argument that Wheadon could earn ten shillings a day.

Meigs wouldn't give up. He told the court that he had no need to use such an argument, "if he did, which possibly he might," for he had "sufficient right" with Wheadon before. The claim that he had promised Wheadon an earning capacity of ten shillings a day had not been proved.

The court had heard enough. It would let the matter of Meigs's exact promise to Wheadon pass. "Precedent things" provided sufficient ground for the court to proceed upon. It announced that Wheadon was no longer bound to Meigs. He must only perform his engagement to Gilbert. The indentures concerning Wheadon were to be kept by the secretary of the colony. Should Meigs subsequently produce additional evidence, the law would be open for his relief.

✦✦✦✦✦

The court's decision in the Currier's Apprentice combines an admirable concern for the plight of an orphan apprentice with an utterly indefensible benefit given to a member of the tribunal. Its recognition that Wheadon, an orphan left alone on a ship bound for a new land, was not in a position to bind himself to servitude for seven years was in the highest tradition of a judicial body that at least occasionally sought to protect those unable to protect themselves. But that, unhappily, is where modern praise of the court's decision must end.

The court's decision that Wheadon was incapable of binding himself to Meigs because he was already bound to an English master—this fact must be the "precedent thing" to which the court referred in its decision—makes some sense as a matter of formal legal reasoning. If Wheadon was already the property of another person, Meigs had no right to take that property without an "assignment" from the owner of the property. But if Wheadon could not bind himself to Meigs for seven years because of his existing legal ties to his English master, how on earth could he nevertheless bind himself to *Gilbert* for five years? Gilbert's only "assignment," if he indeed had any, was from Meigs, and Meigs' "assignment" had just been ruled invalid. The court's noble pronouncement that Wheadon was "a free man" quickly became a mockery. That the court's ruling bound Wheadon to one of its own members for five years was an outrageous act of self-dealing by any standard.

25

❦

THE MILFORD
PATERNITY CASE

❦

Bethia Hawes, an unmarried milkmaid working for a Milford
farmer, was visibly pregnant.[1] John Baldwin, a recently widowed
man residing in the same town, was accused of being the father.
But was this charge true? That was the question confronting the
Court of Magistrates on October 20, 1658.

The Trial: Part 1 (1658)

Hawes and Baldwin, having been warned, were called before the
court. Magistrate Benjamin Fenn declared he had heard it reported that Hawes was with child. She answered that it was so.
She further said that Baldwin was the father, but he denied it. At
this point, Fenn produced the report of two examinations that he
had conducted in Milford earlier in the same month.

At an examination conducted on October 12, Hawes told Fenn
she was with child and that Baldwin was the father. Fenn then
asked whether anyone else had "fellowship" with her "in that way."
She answered that no one had known her in that way but Baldwin, for she was a maid until then. As to when it was done, she

said that it was in April, but what time she could not tell. Asked where it was done, she answered that it was done in her master's yard, "standing up by five [fence] rails." She and Baldwin "were standing all the while." This was, she said, the only "familiarity" between them. She had not received any pledge or item from Baldwin at any time. When asked whether she had been "aboard some vessels," Hawes said that the only vessel she had been on was one belonging to Richard Brian. That had happened twice, in the daytime.

Baldwin denied Hawes's accusations, but Hawes maintained that what she had said was true.

Hawes's employer, Zachariah Whitman, told the magistrate that Hawes might not understand the word "familiarity."

The magistrate asked Baldwin a series of questions. Had he ever kissed Hawes? Baldwin confessed that he had done so. Did he at one time socialize with her? He answered, "Not in any uncivil way." He did, however, have a child "at nurse" (i.e., a child being breastfed by a wet nurse) at Goodwife Denison's, and "as he went that way, she would ask him how the child did."

The magistrate then asked whether Baldwin had not been with her alone. At this point, Whitman interposed, declaring that his wife had found them together in the "old house" or stable; Baldwin confessed to this.

Joseph Peck stated that one evening he came by Whitman's house and there he found Baldwin and Hawes together, with "only the rails between them." This was when Baldwin's child was "at nurse" at the home of Robert Denison.

James Prime testified that one evening, "after daylight was shut in," he saw Baldwin and Hawes together with "only rails between them." Goodwife Prime testified that she had seen the same thing.

Fenn's examination resumed on October 19. Whitman and Peck told Magistrate Fenn that they had wondered several times why Baldwin should be so familiar with Hawes so soon after the death of his wife.

At this point, the magistrate's attention turned to a new suspect in Hawes's pregnancy—one Richard Marshall. Edward Preston testified that he had talked with Marshall, who commended Hawes and added, "He was a fool of a man who could not have the use of a maid, and she not be with child." Edward Turner testified that he had heard Marshall say the same thing.

Sarah Firman and Elizabeth Hinde testified that they had heard Hawes say her brother had sent her a pair of gloves. On further questioning, Hawes admitted that Marshall had given her the gloves.

Hannah Peston testified that, at the beginning of the month, Hawes told her that folks in the town said her stomach was large, but Hawes did not know why her stomach had gotten so big.

Firman testified that Hawes had denied hearing rumors of her pregnancy. When Firman told her that, if she were falsely accused of being pregnant, she would endeavor to clear herself, Hawes answered that she was "clear already."

Hinde testified that she had advised Hawes that, if the report was false, she should tell her master and mistress, and they would seek to clear her. Hawes replied that it was a "lie."

After Magistrate Fenn's examinations had been read in court, Sergeant Richard Baldwin of Milford expressed a desire to speak "though he had no delight in it."[2] Regardless of his lack of delight, Sergeant Baldwin proceeded to act as John Baldwin's spokesman for the remainder of the day. He noted that, although Whitman had told the magistrate that Hawes might not understand the word "familiarity," Hawes had also been asked whether there was any "dalliance" preceding the act. Hawes had answered no. She had also said there was no familiarity between them at any other time.

Fenn responded that John Baldwin had confessed he had kissed Hawes, and that, in Fenn's view, was "dalliance." In addition, several witnesses had said John Baldwin had been "familiar" with her.

Sergeant Baldwin replied that it had been said John Baldwin "had speech" with Hawes as he went to and came from his child. He did not wish to darken the case, but he had something to propound that made the accusation doubtful. Some things that had been said in the magistrate's examination had not been written. Hawes had first said there were no preceding acts of dalliance, only the one act. When asked how long they had been together before the act, she answered that he had newly come into the yard when she was done milking, and then it was done. The magistrate then advised her that, as she had fallen into great sin, she should not add to it by falsely accusing someone to be guilty. When the magistrate demanded to know whether she had used any means to shun him, she answered that she had asked him to be quiet, and he said he would do her no hurt.

Sergeant Baldwin asked the court to consider whether there were not palpable contradictions in some of the testimony given in the magistrate's examinations. Hawes had first said that her brother had sent her a pair of gloves. Afterward she owned them to be the gift of Richard Marshall. Why she should conceal Marshall's name until necessity compelled her, she did not say.

The court asked Hawes for a response to these accusations. She said that she did not remember saying her brother had sent the gloves. They came from the Massachusetts Bay Colony, and Marshall brought them hence.

Whitman stated that, as he took it, Marshall had given her the gloves because he dwelled in Whitman's house and she washed for him. Therefore, he had a right to give her the gloves. She had not concealed the gloves from her mistress. The court declared this ground for giving the gloves to be lawful and honest.

Sergeant Baldwin further said that he could not but marvel that Hawes should say she did not know why her stomach had gotten so big. She had said this not more than a fortnight before the magistrate's examination. Moreover, she had not "scattered such ways of wantonness" only to John Baldwin.

This suggestion of "wantonness" did not go well with the court. If this was true, it responded, it "aggravated his guilt that he would keep company with her at unseasonable times, she being one of so bad a carriage."

Sergeant Baldwin next argued that it had been said Hawes had spoken to sundry women "to speak to some to come a wooing to her." Hawes denied this. Magistrate Fenn admitted that, during the previous examinations, one woman had given testimony to that effect after Hawes had departed. When Fenn sent for Hawes to respond, Hawes said she would not return and that if the woman had anything to say, she might have spoken while Hawes was there.

The court told Hawes that she had spoken falsely. Both she and John Baldwin had "been of a light carriage" with respect to each other.

Sergeant Baldwin admitted that the incident when John Baldwin was in the "old house" with Hawes could not be excused. John had confessed that he was there with her. But Hawes had been milking and, coming by, John had come into her house, which was open. As for the other times spoken of, John was on one side of the rails, and Hawes was on the other. He was passing that way to visit his child, who was "at nurse."

The court responded that Baldwin "might easily pretend occasions," but his behavior had been unsatisfying with respect to Hawes. She was with child, and there was no one to suspect but him.

Sergeant Baldwin replied that there was testimony concerning another man, namely, Richard Marshall. In fact, Sergeant Baldwin had observed such familiarity between Marshall and Hawes that day, in him bringing her from Milford and spending time with her here, as to make him suspicious.

Whitman interposed that Hawes could not ride alone and that Marshall had brought her for this reason. In any event, Marshall had heard that something would be spoken against him in court. If Marshall had been guilty of causing Hawes's pregnancy, he would not have come to Milford in the first place.

The court called Marshall and asked for his response. Marshall replied that the remarks attributed to him by Preston and Turner were base speeches indeed, but he had not spoken them.[3] These witnesses had a grudge against him.

Sergeant Baldwin added that Preston had also said Marshall, who was in charge of a vessel, had admitted leaving the vessel to be at Whitman's house. When Marshall returned, "he was not fit for his business."

The court had heard enough. As for Marshall, it took notice of the base and sinful speeches he had spoken. These words called for corporal punishment, but this being Marshall's first offense, he was sentenced to pay a fine of twenty shillings to the jurisdiction.

Turning to John Baldwin, the court said he had rendered himself a suspicious man with respect to the child's paternity. He confessed he had been with Hawes at unseasonable times and kissed her. She had accused no one else. But the court declared it would wait to see "what the providence of God will discover." In the meantime, it would leave Baldwin as a man under suspicion and require that he post security in the value of fifty pounds out of his land in Milford to attend the court further in this matter when he was called for. (Baldwin posted the security.)

As for Hawes, the court declared she was guilty of a horrible sin, for which she must be held accountable before God and the court. The court told Hawes that she had to deal with an all-seeing God, "who can write her sin in her forehead." This was a jealous God, who would not be dallied with. Whitman assured the court she would appear in court when she was called for.

The Trial: Part 11 (1659)

The case resumed on May 23, 1659. John Baldwin and Hawes were present. Sergeant Richard Baldwin, John Baldwin's spokesman in the first stage of the trial, was not.

The court told John Baldwin that it supposed he remembered what had passed in the first stage of his trial. It then asked him whether he had "anything to say in acknowledgment of his evil."

Baldwin answered that Hawes's charges against him were false.

The court warned Baldwin not to add sin to sin by further denials if he were guilty of what Hawes had charged. She has said these charges and, it is likely, would say them again. In addition, there are "leading circumstances that look that way." But Baldwin remained adamant in pleading not guilty.

The court turned to Hawes. What did she now say to her charges against John Baldwin? Like Baldwin, Hawes was warned not to add sin to sin. If she had falsely charged him, she should now retract it.

Hawes answered that she could say nothing other than what she had already said.

At this point, the court read depositions of Samuel Burrall and Joseph Hakins. Burrall and Hakins testified that, in the winter season, they had seen John Baldwin come in Whitman's house in the evening. Hawes and Baldwin had gone out together and stayed some space of time and then came in together into the house.

The court told Baldwin that it seemed he and Hawes meet and socialize at unseasonable times, as the adulteress that Solomon says walks in the twilight.[4]

Baldwin answered that he had gone to borrow a horse.

The court responded that the two had gone out together and stayed some time. In its opinion, borrowing a horse had been a pretext.

The court then read the testimony of Mrs. Tapp and Mrs. Whitman.[5] These witnesses testified that they were present at Hawes's labor. They heard her say that John Baldwin "had use of her three times." One time was at the stable end, and the other two were against the rails. Hawes further said that Baldwin had torn her coat and said that, if she would bring it to him, he would mend it again.

Magistrate Fenn interposed, stating that Hawes had been delivered before Tapp arrived. The magistrate then requested that an examination of Hawes be read.

In her examination, Hawes testified that she had initially denied "familiarity" with John Baldwin "any more times than one." She had so spoken to make her fault appear less. Asked why she had subsequently said that it was three times, she responded that "she was pressed to it." When asked how long it had been between the times, she said she could not tell. Asked if it was ever after April, she said no. Asked if it was before March, she said yes.

The court told John Baldwin that neither now nor before had he shown sorrow for what had been proven and confessed. It appeared that he had been with Hawes at unseasonable times and that their behavior together had been "unsatisfying." This called for more sorrow than he had expressed before the court. The "common fame [rumor]" said he had acted "with a jolly frame," which rather increased than lessened the suspicion.

The court declared it had heard with grief what had appeared in this matter. Although the "main thing charged" had not been proved, for the things witnessed against Baldwin and confessed by him, it now ordered that he pay a fine to the jurisdiction of forty shillings. In addition, further proceedings could be held "as further discoveries may be made."

As for Hawes, the court looked upon her as "a loose, vain wench, who has been found to be of child." The court sentenced her to be severely whipped, "so as may suit her sex." This was to be done at Milford, "that it may be a warning to any that have had sinful familiarity with her."

⁂

With this ignominious ending, the Milford Paternity Case proves once again that, when it came to sex cases, the standards of justice employed by the Court of Magistrates were vastly different from those recognized in modern times.

This was a paternity case. A modern court hearing a case of this description would, at least initially, want to know the answer to a simple factual question: who was the biological father of the child in question? If the putative father is found to be the biological father, child support will be ordered, for the best interests of the child will be paramount. If the putative father is not the biological father, the case against him must be dismissed.

While the court was undoubtedly interested in the factual

question of biological paternity, its focus centered on the morality of Baldwin and Hawes rather than on biological facts. Some basic questions needed to be asked.[6] When was the child born? Was it full term? When did Hawes have her last period? With the answers to those questions in mind, a probable date of conception can be calculated. The court could then inquire whether any of Baldwin's reported encounters with Hawes occurred at about that time.

Sadly, the child—which had been delivered by the time of the hearing's second stage—is not even mentioned in the records. The court was not only uninterested in the child's date of birth; it was wholly uninterested in the child's existence. Having the child's mother publicly whipped as a warning to others was unlikely to further the child's best interests.

We would also like to know more about Baldwin and Hawes themselves. Baldwin was clearly an adult, for he was a widower, but he might have been young, for he had a nursing child. Was he a widower because his wife died in childbirth? Was he a bereft widower desperate for companionship and comfort, or was he a calculating predator? How old was Hawes? Was she a child or an adult? Significantly, the only person to speak on her behalf was Whitman, her employer. As far as the reports indicate, she had no one else in the world to support her. This adds to the pathos of her story.

The court had no interest in answering these questions. Its focus was entirely different. Its mission was to uphold morality, and to that end it was eager to make examples of the human beings brought before it.

26

⊰⊱

THE BRICKMAKER'S
APPRENTICE

⊰⊱

On October 19, 1659, Samuel Plumb of Branford appeared before the Court of Magistrates asking the court to answer a claim concerning a young apprentice, Edward House.[1] The various proceedings that would eventually result from this claim would reveal a tale of pathetic childhood worthy of Charles Dickens.

The governor, who presided over the court, had received a letter from a Mr. Rawson of Boston complaining that House was being held by Plumb beyond the time expressed in his indenture. House, who was present in court, presented an indenture. The document provided that House, with the consent of his father, was bound to John Strange of Boston from April 19, 1652, for seven years.[2] His servitude was to have ended the previous April.

Plumb countered this evidence with another indenture. This document provided that House had bound himself to one Jeffs for nine years beginning May 1, 1653. The rights to House's servitude had subsequently been traded like a commodity. Jeffs had assigned his rights to one Francis Browne, and Browne had assigned *his* rights to Plumb. According to this document, Plumb had the rights to House's servitude for another three years.

The court asked House how this had come to pass. How had he set his hand to such an indenture?

House answered that he had been forced to sign the second indenture in the ship.[3] He was threatened that he would be thrown overboard if he would not yield to it. Jeffs also told him that if he signed it, he would be allowed to go to sea and see his friends once a year. In addition, Jeffs got House drunk and then forced him to sign the document. This was done when House was twelve or thirteen years old.[4]

The court declared the indenture invalid based on three considerations. First, a child of twelve or thirteen was not capable of making a contract. Second, House had been forced to sign the document. Third, since House's parents were in England, "it cannot be thought rational that he should be left to himself to dispose of himself." It then asked Plumb why he should hold the boy beyond the time expressed in the first indenture.

Plumb answered that he had purchased House's servitude for the time remaining in the 1653 indenture from Francis Browne. This had been done in House's presence, and House had not objected.

The court responded that the indenture itself was invalid. If Browne had committed a wrong to Plumb, Plumb could have justice against Browne, "but the boy must not suffer from it." The governor declared that the court saw no ground for Plumb to hold the boy any longer. The time on the first indenture had expired in April, and the second indenture was invalid. At the first opportunity, at Plumb's expense, House was to be sent to Mr. Rawson to be conveyed to his father in England, "being first furnished with double clothing, according to the custom of the country."

On May 28, 1660, Plumb turned to Francis Browne to seek

recompense. Browne, who lived in Stamford, was bound over to the Court of Magistrates to answer Plumb's claim against him. The proceedings were brief.

One of the parties (it is not clear which) claimed he was not prepared and requested that the proceedings be "respited" (continued) until October. This motion was granted. In the meantime, the security that Browne had already posted at Stamford to guarantee his appearance in court would continue to stand. Jasper Crane, a Branford magistrate, was asked to "have a vigilant eye upon Edward House that he withdraw not" and to ensure that House would attend the court to answer claims that Browne was making against him.

On October 17, 1660, Plumb, Browne, and House appeared before the Court of Magistrates for a final proceeding. The deputy governor presided over the court, the governor being sick.

The deputy governor declared that the governor had received a letter from Mr. Rawson of Boston. The letter complained that House had not been taught the trade of a brickmaker. John Strange of Boston, House's first master, had been engaged to teach him this trade. According to Rawson, House had been held in servitude for eight months beyond the time set by his indenture. The court, however, pointed out that the period of excessive servitude had been six months (from April to October 1659).

Plumb argued that, in lieu of this six months' service, he had been enjoined to transport House to Boston. He would have done so, but House was unwilling to go. House's service had been "worth but little," in any event, since upon his desire, he had "let blood."[5] House had a sore that had festered and had been disabled from service for a month to six weeks. In addition, he had been sick for a fortnight during harvest.

The court asked Plumb and Browne how they had taught House the trade of brickmaking. They could not make it appear that they had taught him anything. According to them, they had not even known that he was to learn the trade.

Plumb added that House was not fit for the trade when Plumb acquired him. He could not bend his knee by reason of scurvy. House had acquired that malady on board ship by eating brewis,[6] his master at the time being the cook. Browne chimed in that House had been so diseased while serving him that he had cost Browne nearly five pounds.

Plumb declared that Browne had sold to him the remainder of House's service under an indenture originally given to Jeffs, which was to be for nine years beginning May 1, 1653. The court declared this indenture invalid in 1659, and House had been set free for his service. For the remaining period of time on the invalid indenture that he had purchased, Plumb demanded that Browne pay him twenty pounds.

Browne acknowledged that he had made the agreement with Plumb. He argued that he was entitled to make the agreement by virtue of House's indenture with Jeffs, although the court had invalidated that document. Browne submitted the case between Plumb and himself to the judgment of the court. He declared, however, that he had received much wrong from Jeffs, from whom he would have to "seek his right as he may." Browne asked the court to consider whether Plumb's demand was "not far above" what the facts justified.

The court declared that it looked upon Browne as having acted imprudently in this matter. It did not, however, see that he had acted fraudulently. It also looked upon House as "under infirmity of body." Given these findings, it ordered that, for the time of

House's service—a service Browne had no right to sell Plumb—Browne must pay Plumb ten pounds within one year as well as court costs of ten shillings.

To discharge this debt, Browne agreed to give Plumb eight pounds in wheat and pease, due from Samuel Steele the next spring and to pay thirty shillings in wampum beads within three months. The security that Browne had posted in Stamford would remain until this was done.

Browne also promised the court that he would submit Rawson's complaint that House had not been taught the trade of brickmaker "to indifferent men to judge" when the court required him to do so, unless Rawson withdrew the claim.

The actions of the court in these proceedings were commendably swift and humane with respect to the young apprentice, Edward House. The court found that House could no longer be held under his indenture and ordered him released. But it also went beyond this initial judicial obligation by apparently taking steps to see that House be taught the trade of brickmaking—the learning requirement that was supposedly the reason for the indenture in the first place. Browne's promise to the court to submit this claim to "indifferent men to judge" suggests that the matter would ultimately be submitted to arbitration in an effort to secure House's occupational future.

The enduring image that lingers from this case, however, is not the case's legal resolution but its pathetic inception. Picture the young House, a boy of twelve or thirteen years, alone on a ship bound from England to the New World. This was not a young man adventurously off to see the world. This was a boy, unaccompanied by his parents, apprenticed for seven years to a man in Boston whom he almost certainly did not know. His master was the ship's cook, who ungenerously fed him a diet rivaling that of Oliver Twist. Instead of thin gruel, House was forced to subsist on bread soaked in fat. As a result, he developed scurvy.

Starving and malnourished, House was given liquor and forced to sign an even more onerous indenture on threat of being thrown overboard. Arriving on land, he was sold from owner to owner like a sack of wheat or, more accurately, a slave. He was bled, which undoubtedly made his medical condition worse. He had a sore that festered. He was so diseased that he was hardly fit for service.

When we think of the immigrants who populated the New World, we think of paintings depicting intrepid pioneers and earnest pilgrims in search of economic and religious freedom. Many such archetypes doubtless existed. But the Brickmaker's Apprentice reminds us that there were other immigrants as well—abandoned and malnourished children bound to harsh and unscrupulous masters who robbed them of their health and youth and sold them like slaves. The Court of Magistrates recognized that House had the rights to freedom and vocational training. Regardless of the court's faults in other cases, it deserves commendation here.

27

THE

HORSE-TRADING

CASE

It turns out that Francis Browne—one of the villains in the Brick-maker's Apprentice—didn't deal only in malnourished appren-tices.[1] He was also a horse trader in the literal sense of the word, and no more ethical in the sale of horses than of human beings. The Court of Magistrates found this out on October 17, 1660, shortly after the Brickmaker's Apprentice had been concluded.

John Archer of Stamford appeared before the court with the following story.[2] In February 1659, Archer had a horse that Browne wished to purchase. After some negotiation, they agreed that Archer would give Browne the horse in return for either "his choice of Francis Browne's horses or thirteen pounds in pease and wheat." Archer delivered the horse to Browne.

Archer was afraid that the grain harvest would fall short, so he decided to take the alternative payment of a horse. But instead of a choice from all of his horses, Browne presented a single two-year-old horse, telling Archer that if he didn't like the horse he would have to keep it until his other horses "came up."[3] Archer didn't like the deal and commenced this suit.

Archer presented his case to the court in the form of four written "testimonies" taken in Stamford on October 13 and 15.

William Newman, "aged about 50 years," testified that he had heard Archer and Browne make their bargain. Browne said, "If you will let me have your bay horse you bought of Goodman Stokey, I will let you have the choice of my horses or thirteen pounds in pease and wheat." This was in the winter of 1659. Later, after Newman had heard that the bargain had been broken, he met with the parties individually, and they told him they had only broken the bargain with respect to the wheat and pease. The choice about the horses stood.

Cornelius Jones testified that Archer was to have the choice of all of Browne's horses in return for the horse that Archer had purchased from Goodman Stokey. Jones heard Browne say that Archer was to "have the choice of all his horses." If the horses did not content Archer, then Browne would pay him thirteen pounds in pease and wheat in the spring of 1660.

Richard Ambler testified that, in his presence, Browne had said "Archer was to have the choice of all his horses."

Stephen Clawson testified that Archer and Browne had discoursed about the horse in his presence. Browne told Archer he "should have the choice of all their horses, that was his bargain."

Browne admitted to the court that he had a horse of the plaintiff's. Although his fancy had led him to the horse, it had fallen sick while he was riding to Norwalk and was so tired that he was forced to drag it five miles. He had kept the horse all winter. In May, he offered the horse back to Archer, but Archer refused to accept it. The terms of the agreement were that Archer "was to have his choice of a horse when they came up." To prove this, Browne offered three written testimonies of his own.

Joseph Meade, "aged about 30 years," testified that Archer told him that he had given his best horse to Browne, and "he was to have one of the best of his horses when they came up." This testimony was corroborated by Francis's wife, Martha, and by Thomas Browne, "aged about 22."[4]

Francis Browne told the court that he had used all possible means to find his horses. Jonathan Lockwood and Meade affirmed that they had, at Browne's request, spent money to find horses to suit Archer but could not find them.

Browne further told the court that he had offered Archer an "ambling horse" (i.e., a horse moving at an easy pace) that he had ridden on, but the horse was not accepted. He had also offered a black horse and forty shillings in corn. He had further offered to take the black horse back when he found his other horses and then give Archer his choice. In support of this, Browne offered the written testimony of Richard Law.

Law testified that, in his presence, Browne had offered Archer a black horse, which by Law's estimation, was fully as good as the horse Archer had given to Browne. Browne had also offered forty shillings to be paid in corn. Browne had additionally promised that, if Archer could not "make his market" of the black horse, Browne would take back the black horse, and Archer "should have his choice of other horses."

Archer admitted that a horse had been offered but said it was not worth seven pounds at market.

Meade responded that "the horse was a substantial, well grown horse."

Archer further said that, when Browne did not present him with a horse to his satisfaction, he agreed to accept twelve pounds of wheat and pease in March. Browne would not consent to that resolution but offered to pay four of the twelve pounds in Indian corn. Archer wouldn't agree to that, so now he expected his choice of horse, according to the original agreement.

Browne told the court that he had used all means to achieve a quiet and peaceable end. He had made all manner of tender and had additionally offered to refer the case to the judgment of impartial men. In support of this last statement, he submitted the written testimony of Robert Poynere, who said that Browne had offered to put the case "to any indifferent men to judge what was right between them, and he would stand by their judgment" but that Archer had refused.

The court told Archer that, if Browne could not get up all his horses, why should not a "composition" be made such as the one Browne had offered, namely, a black horse and forty shillings in corn? The horse, by one witness, was said to be a "substantial, well grown horse," as good as the horse Archer had given Browne.

The deputy governor, speaking for the court, declared that it did not see cause to require Browne to pay damages in the action, "for that the time for payment seems not to be expired." But, so due payment might be made, the court ordered that Browne use all reasonable and honest endeavors to find as many of his horses as may be had within four months and present them to Archer, so he could choose one to his best content. If the horses were found and presented gradually, Archer could refuse a horse and later change his mind. In that case, the horse would have to be retrieved at Archer's expense, but only if impartial men valued it at twelve pounds. Browne was required to have one horse in hand at all times until the end of the four-month period.

The Horse-Trading Case presented the court with a recurring problem in the law of contracts. What does a court do when it becomes impossible or impractical to perform a contract? Although classic contract doctrine has always encouraged the strict performance of contracts, judicial doctrine has not been entirely inflexible. If the performance of a contract proves to be impossible or unreasonable, courts have always been willing to step in. For example, a sixteenth-century English judge said that if a man agreed to provide a person to sing in St. Paul's Cathedral and the church fell down, he was not bound to rebuild the cathedral.[5]

Modern contract law focuses on the basic assumptions of the parties at the time of the contract. If a party's performance is made impracticable by the occurrence of an event and the nonoccurrence of the event was a "basic assumption" on which the contract was made, a modern court will nullify the contract.[6] If, for example, a company agrees to work on a building and the building burns down before the work can be done, the contract will be rescinded.[7] When the parties made the contract, they obviously assumed the building would be around long enough to be repaired. If they had known that the building was about to burn down, they wouldn't have made the contract in the first place. The idea is to interpret the contract in a reasonable way.

In ordering the remedy that it did in the Horse-Trading Case, the court was obviously trying to interpret the parties' intent in a reasonable way. But it should have asked some more questions. To use the parlance of Watergate, what did Browne know, and when did he know it? If he knew when he made the contract with Archer that he wouldn't have a "choice" of horses available when Archer made good his part of the bargain, he should have told Archer that fact. Otherwise, Browne was simply deceiving Archer, and the court, with its moralistic agenda, should have found such behavior unacceptable.

What if Browne could *not* have known that his horses would be unavailable when it came time for Archer to make his choice? If this was an eventuality that could not reasonably have been anticipated by the contracting parties, the court should also have considered the possibility of simply nullifying the entire contract and requiring Browne to return the original (Stokey) horse to Archer. While that solution would have deprived Archer the benefit of his bargain, it would also have recognized that the bargain probably would not have been made in the first place if this eventuality had been known. In that case, it would be fair to restore the parties to their original (precontract) positions.

The complicated solution the court arrived at was arguably fair as well, but a few additional questions would have led to a more just resolution.

28

⋙≋⋘

THE MILFORD
ARSON CASE

⋙≋⋘

On December 11, 1660, the Court of Magistrates was presented with another case involving a young servant and a harsh master.[1] In this case, the young servant found little sympathy in the court.

Jacobus Loper, a twelve-year-old servant to Hans Albers, a "Dutchman" living in Milford, was accused of first setting fire to a house inhabited by a man named John Baldwin and then, a few days later, setting fire to a house inhabited by Albers.

Loper was examined by a magistrate and initially confessed that he had committed the crimes. When asked for details, he then denied the crimes outright. He subsequently said that some seamen had come to the door when his master was in bed and offered to give him a pistol, powder, and ribbons if he would set fire to Baldwin's house. Loper then changed his story again and said that he had carried a coal out to the fence rails. The seamen had taken it and joined him in setting fire to the house. At last, Loper "wholly freed the seamen" and confessed that he had done it himself by setting fire to a clapboard on the outside of the house.

Loper also told the magistrate his reasons for setting fire to the clapboard. First, he thought it might burn down his master's house as well and thereby free him from service to go home to his mother. Second, Baldwin, who lived in the house, had complained to Loper's master that he had stolen Baldwin's plums. For that, he had been beaten.

The magistrate sent Loper to the prison in New Haven. He was then called before the court.

The court told Loper that he was accused of a notorious crime. Being a servant to Albers, he had taken his time to set fire to Baldwin's house, a fire that had consumed the house and all that was in it. A lengthy dialogue followed.

> COURT: Was this so?
>
> LOPER: No.
>
> COURT: You have confessed it, only you vary in the manner. Have you not confessed that you did it by the instigation of some seamen?
>
> LOPER: Yes.
>
> COURT: What had moved you to it? How did it first begin to work in your thoughts?
>
> LOPER: As I was going by [Baldwin's house] in the day, I heard that John Baldwin would not be there at night. In the night, as I was passing by, I heard a noise in the house and went in. Finding some seamen, I asked what they did there. They said if I would swear not to tell (which I did) I would know. Then they said if I would set fire to one end of the house, they would set fire to the other, and I did so.
>
> COURT: What was the reason that you did this wicked act?
>
> LOPER: Because John Baldwin had complained to my master that I had stolen his plums, for which I was beaten.

COURT: Whither were you going so late?

LOPER: My master being in bed with a stranger, I had to lie by the fire.[2] I went toward Mr. Fenn's to play.

COURT: Where did you start the fire?

LOPER: On a corner of the house that was burnt.

COURT: Were any appointed to play with you?

LOPER: No. Nor did I know that anybody was in the house until I heard the noise as I was going by.

COURT: How many seamen were there?

LOPER: I thought there were six, but I knew none of them.

COURT: Why do you lay it upon the seamen now, having formerly said that you did it yourself? Why did you not accuse them at first?

LOPER: I was afraid the seamen would kill me.

COURT: Why have you told these several stories? Which is the truth?

LOPER: The truth is that which I have now related.

COURT: You have said that the seamen gave you ribbons. What became of the ribbons?

LOPER: I gave them away.

COURT: You said that these ribbons were given you by your mother, and John Baldwin testified that he had them long before.

LOPER: The seamen gave them to me.

COURT: You had said that there were but four seamen and that they came to the door when your master was in bed.

LOPER: That was untrue.

COURT: From the first to the last you have confessed that you did it or had a hand in it, one time saying that when your master was in bed four seamen came to the door, and another time that you heard the seamen make a noise in the house as you were going by to Mr. Fenn's to play. Take it either way, you always confess that you either did it or had a hand in it. Your reason is that John Baldwin complained to your master of the matter of the plums, which complaint was likely true and the correction just. You have nothing to say against your master for any ill usage, as you have acknowledged. You are reported to be a notorious, lying boy, a great offense to the English amongst whom you live, and a dishonor to the nation to which you belong, and you have perpetrated this act costing a great sum which you are not able to pay.

John Baldwin presented an account of goods in his house belonging to several Milford residents. He asked that they might be "righted" for the damage to their goods, which amounted to about seventy-eight pounds. In addition, about eight or ten pounds worth of goods belonged to Mrs. Tapp.

George Clark, the owner of Baldwin's house, informed the court that his house was worth thirty pounds and he also lost a piece of serge fabric worth about three pounds, but he did not now demand damages.

The court asked Loper if he had seen these goods in the house or had seen them conveyed away by the seamen.

Loper replied that he had not seen the goods. The seamen went over the lots behind his master's house, but they carried away no goods that he saw. He also did not hear from them why they wanted to set fire to the house, nor did he know what became of the goods or of any complaint about them.

The court had heard enough. It found that Loper had criminally burned one house to the ground and afterward attempted to burn his master's house. To these offenses, he had added many lies. For these miscarriages, the court ordered that he be corporally punished by whipping. Second, since he had by these acts brought damage upon others that, in addition to the house, was to the value of about one hundred pounds (the proof is left to the judgment of the court at Milford), it was ordered that Loper pay double or to the satisfaction of those who would prove their damage by the fire. If Loper or others on his behalf did not satisfy this amount, he was to be "sold for a servant." Third, so that the court's jurisdiction in the future would be secured, it was ordered that whoever kept Loper should post security for "future damage by such like mischievous attempts of his." Loper was to remain in the marshal's custody until this sentence was fulfilled.

On May 17, 1661, Sergeant Richard Baldwin and some other Milford creditors appeared before the court to prosecute Loper for a debt.[3] The creditors had attached Loper's blanket and pillow; theses pathetic articles were supposed to be the boy's "estate." The court told Baldwin that "the boy was much indebted to the jurisdiction, which must be first paid." The deputy governor added that Loper "hath been kept in prison to this time to see if any would appear on his behalf, to satisfy for the wrong done, but none hath appeared."

Baldwin declared that the damage sustained by the creditors was very great. He asked that the court try harder to realize some money from the boy's services by sending him to Barbados.

The court told Baldwin it was not inclined to this extreme measure, but it did order that Loper remain in prison until he had achieved the correction formerly ordered and then be delivered to his master, Hans Albers, who was to "convey him out of the jurisdiction." The bolster and the blanket were to remain under custody until Loper's debt was satisfied.

⬧⬧⬧⬧⬧⬧

Why was a court that, just a year earlier, had been so solicitous of the rights of a young servant in the Brickmaker's Apprentice now so oblivious to the plight of the even younger Jacobus Loper? The formal answer, of course, is that Loper had committed a criminal act, and Edward House, the brickmaker's apprentice, was blameless. But reading between the lines, it is blindingly obvious that the Milford Arson Case involved something other than the calculated acts of a hardened criminal.

The facts of this case are pathetic. Loper was a twelve-year-old boy. He wanted to go home to his mother. He had only a blanket and a bolster to his name. Instead of having a protective and nur-turing parent, he had a master who beat him for stealing plums. An experienced modern judge looking at these facts would likely conclude that the fires set by Loper (assuming that he was, indeed, the arsonist) were cries for attention and help. Because the best interests of the child guide modern law pertaining to juveniles, a modern judge would be obliged to look to Loper's best interests in reaching an appropriate disposition of the case. This would not preclude appropriate punishment for criminal acts, but a modern-day Loper would also be entitled to receive the help he so obviously needed.

The court's resolution of the case was, in contrast, appalling. Loper was denounced as "a dishonor to the nation," whipped, ordered to pay a total of two hundred pounds in double damages, sent out of the jurisdiction, and sold into servitude until this impossible amount was paid. A twelve-year-old boy who longed for his mother and had been beaten for stealing plums was thus essentially to be sold as a slave.

The outcome of this case is analogous to that of the Farmhand Arsonist in 1656. Perhaps the twelve-year-old Loper, as with the fourteen-year-old John Frost, was fortunate in that he was not hanged (or, in Loper's case, sent to Barbados, which might have been a de facto death sentence). But the practice of selling troubled children into servitude stands as an indelible black mark on the record of the court.

29

THE SOUTHOLD SLANDER

On May 27, 1661, a case from Southold found its way to New Haven.[1] Captain John Young brought an action in the Court of Magistrates against Lieutenant John Budd for slander.

Young charged that Budd had come into the local court at Southold and said, "We was very strict against Quakers, but we could suffer [tolerate] whoring and drinking or drunkenness."

Budd told Young to prove his charge. At this point, William Wells said that Budd's statement had been made to the entire court and "therefore every one took it particularly to himself."

Young added that Budd had several times charged him with lying when Young had told Budd that "he tended to disturb the peace."

Budd responded to Young's first charge with a qualified apology. "Sir, I have acknowledged them to be hasty words. The words were 'whoring, tippling, and wantonness.'" As to Young's second charge, Budd said that he had been brought into church about the matter and had given satisfaction to those who were there. For three-quarters of a year after that, he had communion with the church members at the Lord's table.

Wells told the court that the people of Southold had tried to "reclaim" Budd in another way by using his son to persuade him to come and make acknowledgment of his evil.

Budd's initial response was vehement. "You dealt with me as a rogue, binding me over to appear in a bond of one hundred pounds." But he then acknowledged that the words charged had been spoken by him and that they were evil words, passed from him in haste and distemper. He confessed that he had cast a "reproach" upon the members of the Southold court and had "slandered them all."

Wells told the court that he saw Budd as "something pliable" and that he was not willing to bring further trouble upon him. He noted that, in one of Budd's writings, he had said he was a "wretched man" who was "undone" in body and soul. The Southold court had publicly said much to Budd "to convince him of his evil."

Budd answered, "As the Lord sets it upon my heart, I shall acknowledge it."

Magistrate Robert Treat, a member of the Court of Magistrates, counseled Budd to petition for mercy "in a free acknowledgment of his evil."

Lieutenant Charles Glover now chimed in. Glover wished to say two things to Budd, emphasizing that it was not his money that the members of the Southold court desired. First, Budd had come into the Southold court saying that Glover "had taken away his place from him." Second, Budd "went about to take his head."[2]

Budd initially denied making these statements, but the marshal of Southold testified that Budd had indeed uttered these words. Budd then acknowledged that his first statement was an "evil speech" and that Lieutenant Glover had never sought his place nor was he capable of doing so.

Magistrate Treat advised Budd to give "all encouragement" to soldiers to obey their present officers. Budd then acknowledged the evil of his second speech and said he was sorry for it.

At this point, the court read a deposition under oath by Glover taken in open court in Southold on July 20, 1660. Glover testified that he had occasionally been in Budd's house, discoursing on some points of religion. When the topic of the Quakers came up, Budd commended them, saying they were "the honestest and most godly people that were now in the world." Budd said that he greatly disliked governmental proceedings against the Quakers and that "they would one day have cause to repent thereof." He asked Glover "why they might not have liberty here as well as in other countries," saying that they were not similarly abused where they came from, as they were here. Glover told Budd that he was much mistaken, but Budd replied that the Quakers were such a people that he wished he was worthy to lay down his life for them and would do so if he were called to it.

Wells added that a Dutchman named Clause had also been present when Budd made these statements, although (presumably because of language difficulties) Clause had not fully understood the remarks.

Hearing this, Budd said that Glover was "a false fellow" for making his sworn statement. This charge "much unsatisfied" Glover.

The governor, presiding over the court, told Budd he was "a Quaker in heart and affection" and "among the generation spoken of in Jude that speaks evil of dignities."[3] In the governor's view, Young would prove that Budd favored the Quakers.

Several people spoke in rapid succession.

YOUNG: It will be proved that the Quakers preached in his house, both men and women.

BUDD: It was without my consent.

GOVERNOR: Do you acknowledge your evil about the Quakers?

YOUNG: I heard him commend them.

BUDD: They held forth Christ in their speeches.

COURT: It appears by these things that you carried too friendly to the Quakers.

BUDD: The speech I spoke against Lt. Glover was very evil. I had no ground to speak so of him.

Having heard Budd's acknowledgment, the court was prepared to pass sentence. It declared that Budd's carriage in these things had been very bad and that he had greatly slandered Captain Young. If Budd had not shown his "moderation" to the court, he would have been more severely "witnessed against," but because of his acknowledgment of his evil, he was ordered to pay Young ten pounds and the costs of the action.

As for Budd's "other miscarriages," in his "troublesome miscarriage at Southold," so much testified to here, and in his speeches about the Quakers, "wherein it's to be feared that he hath cast an aspersion on the governments," he was sentenced to pay a fine of five pounds to the jurisdiction. The court additionally left Budd a "serious warning that he be not found in such ways again." If he was, "it would be much heavier upon him than this time."

As for the "business about Mr. Wells," the court left the matter to Budd "seriously to consider of and make up with him."

Budd had the final word. As things had been presented, "he saw not how the court could do less."

The Southold Slander shows the Court of Magistrates reverting to the totalitarian form it so characteristically displayed in cases involving religious belief. Authorities, judicial and religious alike, were not to be questioned. No "aspersion" was to be cast on government. Members of the community were to act as "soldiers" obeying their "officers." Quaker services were to be suppressed. Persons expressing sympathy with the Quakers were told to publicly repent their "evil" or face heavy punishment. In cases of this description, the court forthrightly acted as an instrument of repression.

30

꙰꙰꙰

THE
BIGAMIST'S
WIFE

꙰꙰꙰

On October 16, 1661, Mary Andrews came before the Court of Magistrates, asking to be "freed from her husband."[1] She told the following tale.

Mary Andrews was the wife of William Andrews Jr. She had heard that her husband was married to another woman. For proof of her claim, she presented two letters. One letter was from Nathaniel Whitfield in England. The second was from Richard Miles Jr. "out of Barbados." The letter from Miles, however, was torn, and the court asked Mary to call Miles himself so that it might hear what he could say. It turned out that Miles was in New Haven rather than Barbados anyway, so he was called before the court and placed under oath.

Miles testified that in September 1660, he had been in Barbados. While there, he saw William Andrews, who belonged to a small vessel named the *Charles*. The master of the *Charles* was Robert Guardus. Guardus told Miles that Andrews was married to one Joan King, a Cornish woman then living in Kinsale, Ireland. Miles asked Guardus if he was certain of the thing.

Guardus responded that he was sure, for he was Andrews's "near neighbor."

Miles then spoke to Andrews. After some discourse, he asked Andrews about reports that he was married to a woman in Ireland. At first, Andrews denied this, but when Miles responded that Guardus had told him it was true and had given Miles her name, Andrews became "much amazed." For a while, he scarcely spoke a word, but eventually he confessed that he was "married to one in Ireland" and was "an undone man."

Mary Andrews told the court that her husband had been absent from New England about eight or nine years. He had had "sundry opportunities of returning back to her" but had never done so to this day.

Thomas Kemberly informed the court that his son had written from Bristow, Virginia, that he had heard William Andrews was married in Ireland and that he had written to Andrews that his wife was alive in New England.

The court, considering the evidence and the long time of William Andrews's absence from his wife, saw "no cause to keep Mary Andrews in bonds to such a man." It declared her to be divorced from him and that "she was fully at liberty to marry another without offense."

⊰⊱⊰⊱

This modest little case is something of a landmark in American jurisprudence. With no discoverable authority allowing it to do so, a seventeenth-century court granted a full divorce to a wronged woman on what might fairly be called humanitarian grounds.

A brief sketch of the legal backdrop to Mrs. Andrews's petition explains the exceptional nature of the relief granted by the court. The biblical law that in theory governed the court did not allow divorce. "What therefore God hath joined together, let not man put asunder" (Matthew 19:6). The contemporary law of England was hardly more promising. The law of the Middle Ages remained in place. Full divorces allowing remarriage were not available in England. The best legal arrangement available was a separation from bed and board without the privilege of remarriage. It might occasionally happen that, with a wink and a nod, a *husband* might be allowed remarriage after a judicial separation for a wife's adultery, but that was about it.[2] For a wronged *wife* to receive a similar indulgence would be quite extraordinary.

The court based its decision to allow Mary Andrews the right to remarry on desertion rather than bigamy. In doing so, it implicitly realized that the issue of the husband's bigamy was a red herring in the context of Mrs. Andrews's petition. Bigamy was a crime,[3] not a ground for divorce. By the ecclesiastical law of England, a second marriage, entered into while a former spouse was still living, was "simply void and a mere nullity."[4] So if any marriage were to be set aside on the ground of bigamy, it would be William Andrews's *second* marriage, not his *first*.

A nullification of William Andrews's second marriage, however, would simply leave his first marriage intact, and that would be an injustice to Mary Andrews. Her husband had vanished for years and neither loved her nor supported her. If her marriage had been left legally intact, she could not remarry. While she had managed to live without a husband for eight or nine years, this situation could probably not have continued indefinitely. For economic reasons she might have been forced to live in an unsanctified relationship with another man or become dependent on the colony, and neither alternative was likely to be attractive to the court. On both practical and humanitarian grounds, the court's bold decision to grant her a full divorce was justified.

31

THE STAMFORD MURDER MYSTERY

John Whitmore of Stamford was dead, and an Indian had killed him.[1] That much was clear to the Court of Magistrates. But who, exactly, was the killer? The defendant, an Indian named Taphanse, had long "lay under a suspicion of being guilty." Taphanse, however, said that the real killer was another Indian named Taquatoes. The court took up this matter on October 15, 1662. There were to be many twists and turns along the way.

Taphanse was brought before the court, which (we learn later) had traveled to Stamford to hear the case. The governor said that, by taking flight, the defendant had evaded coming to trial, but having lately received intelligence of his whereabouts, the governor had ordered his apprehension. The arrest had been made, and Taphanse had "been kept in durance for some space of time."

An interpreter was present and informed Taphanse of why he was there.

Taphanse had previously been examined in Stamford, and an account of the brief examination was read:

QUESTION: Are you guilty or not guilty of the death of John Whitmore?

ANSWER: Not guilty.

QUESTION: Why did you fly away?

ANSWER: I did not run away but was sent to the place where the murderer was and did not at all run away.

The governor then told Taphanse that his answer at the Stamford examination was not what he had heard, namely, that Taphanse, being with some others, had "given them the slip." Taphanse answered that he wanted to be cleared. In response, two written testimonies were read.

John Mead, in a sworn statement signed at Stamford on July 2, 1662, testified that he had been at Goodman Richard Law's house about sunrise on the second morning after Goodman Whitmore was reported missing. Shortly afterward, Taphanse came in and told Law that Ponas had sent him and that an Englishman had been killed. Law asked him where the Englishman had been killed. Taphanse answered that he did not know how far off, whether ten, twenty, or thirty miles, but pointed and said it was up the river. Law asked him what Indian had killed the man. Taphanse said it was an Indian who lived up near the Mohawks and that the Indian told him and his companions at their wigwams that he would kill an Englishman. They offered the Indian wampum not to do it, but he refused and went away very angry.

When Goodman Law further questioned Taphanse, he said that this Indian, whom he now named Taquatoes, went away in haste and left a stocking at their wigwams. Law said he would go with Taphanse to the wigwams, and as they were going, he trembled and shook so that several people took notice and said that "his carriage argued guilt." When they came to the wigwam, Taphanse showed them the stocking and then slipped into a wigwam. He then went from wigwam to wigwam and so slipped away. He did not return to help look for Whitmore's killer as he had promised to do at Law's house, although several other Indians came to help them look.

Richard Ambler in a sworn statement, signed on May 2, 1662, affirmed that he had come with Goodman Jessop to Goodman Law's house on the morning that Taphanse brought the news of an Englishman being killed. Law asked Taphanse how he knew there was an Englishman killed. Taphanse answered that there was an Indian at their wigwams before who had said he would kill an Englishman. After he had killed him, the Indian came again and brought with him a shirt and a pair of stockings. Some of these things were bloody.

Taphanse promised to return with them to the wigwams. In going, he was very fearful and trembled and quaked much, so that the rest took great notice of it. Many of them, including Law, said they thought Taphanse was "guilty of the blood of the man." When they came to the wigwams, Taphanse showed them a stocking that he said Taquatoes had left there. Notwithstanding his promise to return with them, he gave them the slip. Several other Indians came to help look for the man. The stocking that Taphanse showed them was bloody.

TAPHANSE: I am not guilty of these things. I deny running away and further deny "those things about the stockings." After this incident I went further up into the country.

GOVERNOR: One time, Uncas had been sent to seek the dead body. You had been with him and some other Indians. As they were roasting venison, You went a little from them and ran away, so that Uncas brought word that you were missing.

TAPHANSE: It was so, and I did very ill in so doing.

Court: What was your reason for doing this?

TAPHANSE: An Indian came and told me that Uncas would take me and carry me away and told me to run away, and so I did.

COURT: Why should you run away more than another Indian if you were innocent?

TAPHANSE: If I knew myself guilty, I would speak, but I was afraid and therefore did fly. I am sorry I did so, for I did evil and gave just cause of suspicion.

COURT: How did you know that Taquatoes did the murder, because you always said this? Were you by?

TAPHANSE: I heard it from an Indian. The Sachem of Croton [Croton-on-Hudson, New York] sent an Indian to Ponas the day after John Whitmore was killed to tell us an Englishman was killed. It was about sunset, and they advised me not to come to tell the English the next morning.

COURT: Croton was about forty miles thence. How Taquatoes could do this murder that day and afterward go to Croton, seeing that it was about eleven o'clock when John Whitmore went out of Stamford, and then send down this word the next day to Ponas?

TAPHANSE: It is not half a day's journey if I stir betimes.

COURT: Did you see Taquatoes the day John Whitmore was killed?

TAPHANSE: Two days before he was at Norwalk, and I saw him there, but whether he went I know not, and I know nothing of his intention. I give you my heart in this.

COURT: Were you at John Whitmore's house the day he was killed?

TAPHANSE: No, nor at Stamford all that day.

COURT: Where were you then?

TAPHANSE: At my father's, making wampum.

The court now read the written testimony of Anne Akerly, taken on July 2, 1662. Akerly testified that she was a widow of about seventy-five years. On the day that Goodman Whitmore was killed, a little in the afternoon, she saw the Indian called Taphanse at Goodman Whitmore's house with other Indians. Taphanse shook the wife of Goodman Whitmore by the hand and asked her where her husband[2] was, for he "so big loved" her husband. She replied that she could not tell.

COURT: Upon hearing this, Goodwife Whitmore was in such an ecstasy [excitement] that she feared some mischief had befallen her husband. Several people at Stamford have said the same that Goodwife Whitmore has said, Taphanse lies in this business.

TAPHANSE: What shall I say if testimony comes in against me? If I speak the truth, I must say I was not there. It was a mistake. She would not speak it to my face. If Manatue were here, he would say the same as I do.

INTERPRETER: He spoke in a phrase that noted his confirmation of this as more than ordinary.

COURT: Knowing that you and Taquatoes were under suspicion in this business, you saw Taquatoes at Stamford last winter and yet did not disclose him, which might have been a fair way to have cleared yourself, but you hid the guilty person.

TAPHANSE: It is very true that might make me suspicious, but the English never spoke to me to do it. If I had done it,

it would have been a fair way to clear myself. I confess I did
foolishly.

COURT: How did you come to go so readily to the place when
they went to look for the body, when you had appeared to
know nothing?

TAPHANSE: I knew it well enough, for Taquatoes told me the
very piece of ground.

COURT: How did you come to know it?

TAPHANSE: Mr. Law sent me to know it of Taquatoes. Being
at the Mattatucks, I was weary and so sent by an Indian to
wish Taquatoes to meet me there. So he did, and he told me
the place. Many English here know the murderer. Neither
English nor Indian could say that two people killed the man.

COURT: Do you have anything else to say?

TAPHANSE: All I have to say is I am innocent.

COURT: How did you come to have such correspondence with
Taquatoes about this thing more than another Indian?

TAPHANSE: Mr. Law sent me to know it of Taquatoes.

COURT: Are the Indians at the Mattatucks friends to
Taquatoes?

TAPHANSE: It is all one, his own country.

INTERPRETER: I have often been among the Indians when
mischief was done among the English, and those Indians
that were innocent would tremble with fear.

After considering the case, the governor, in the name of the
court, declared that it appeared to the court, "and to all standers
by against him," that Taphanse was, by his own acknowledgment,
"suspected of being accessory to this man's murder." The grounds
of this suspicion were his trembling and his slipping away contrary

to his promise of help. In addition, he had lied about the stockings. There was also testimony that he had been at Whitmore's house that day "in such a fawning way." The coming of Taquatoes to meet Taphanse at the Mattatucks showed "correspondence" with him. Taphanse's failure to discover Taquatoes when he was at Stamford, when he had a duty to clear himself of suspicion of guilt, was also considered.

On the whole, the governor explained, "there stands a blot upon him of suspicion," and there was sufficient ground for his apprehension and commitment to "durance" (jail). All that Taphanse had said could not "clear him of a stain of suspicion." But as to his being guilty of the murder, either directly or as an accessory, the governor pronounced him "not guilty in point of death."

At the same time, the governor declared, Taphanse stood bound to pay all charges in the case and was left "guilty of suspicion."[3] He stood bound to "his duty to do his best endeavor to obtain the murderer." He was to remain in custody until the next session of the court, about a fortnight hence, unless he gave some assurance of paying the assessed charge, which the court concluded to be ten pounds.

Taphanse answered that he would do his "utmost endeavor" to procure Taquatoes and pay the charge, but he was poor. He would send to his friends to see what could be done, but he desired that his chain be taken off. The court responded that then he would run away.

Taphanse answered this concern with an ingenious suggestion. He proposed that if he ran away, the court could consider his flight a confession of guilt and, in that eventuality, "they should kill him."

The proposal was accepted. Taphanse was granted his liberty and ordered to appear at the next meeting of the court. He promised to do so, although he could not obtain the money.

A subsequent notation in the records indicates that the "charges" of the court were never paid. One of these charges was a sum of five pounds paid to a marshal for keeping Taphanse in his custody for about seventeen weeks. In addition, on May 6, 1663, the General Court of the colony considered how to pay "the charges expended in the magistrates going to Stamford and keeping court there, seeing that part of their time was spent about the Indian Taphanse." The General Court ordered that one-third of those charges were to be borne by the colony, and the remaining two-thirds were to be paid by the Town of Stamford.

Taphanse never paid any of the charges imposed on him. We never hear of him or Taquatoes again.

⋙⋘

The Stamford Murder Mystery remains a mystery today. We don't know who killed Whitmore. We don't know what became of Taphanse or Taquatoes. And we don't know what the court could possibly have been thinking when it resolved the case as it did.

There was nothing wrong with the court's official verdict of "not guilty." The murky facts presented in the records leave no more than a bare suspicion that Taphanse was guilty of the crime. Under these circumstances, "not guilty" was the only possible verdict.

At least officially, the court agreed. Although there was a "stain of suspicion" upon Taphanse, the court pronounced him "not guilty." Having said this, however, it ordered him to pay the court's charges and left him "guilty of suspicion." By any known standard of criminal justice, this was an extraordinary decision. Writing a century later, William Blackstone expressed the long-held understanding of the Anglo-American justice system. If a defendant is found not guilty, "he is then forever quit and discharged of the accusation."[4] The purpose of this requirement is obvious. If a defendant could be acquitted and thereafter be officially labeled a "suspicious" person and liable to pay the costs of the court to boot, one might legitimately ask what the trial was supposed to be for in the first place.

The most stunning aspect of the case, however, is the court's postverdict decision to release Taphanse on his agreement to the condition that, if he ran away, he could be killed without further process of law. This amazing condition created a potential *Hunger Games* scenario that could serve nicely as the plot of a suspense film but had plenty of jurisprudential problems nevertheless. Bail decisions are ordinarily made before trial rather than after an acquittal. After an acquittal, a defendant is free to go. But regardless of the stage of the proceedings, a legal arrangement leaving a defendant subject to summary execution, presumably by any vigilante on the street, is an arrangement antithetical to the very idea of law. This unusual decision also gave Taphanse a perverse incentive to leave the jurisdiction as quickly as possible. Remaining in a jurisdiction while subject to summary execution does not sound like a healthy alternative.

꧁꧂

32

THE LECHEROUS

SWINEHERD

꧁꧂

We last met John Frost in 1656 as the Farmhand Arsonist.[1] A fourteen-year-old farmhand at the time, he was sentenced to a severe whipping and twenty-one years of servitude for starting a fire that led to the burning of a dwelling. Six years later, Frost, now a swineherd, was in trouble again. On October 15, 1662, following the trial of the Stamford Murder Mystery, Frost was brought before the Court of Magistrates charged with serious sexual crimes against children.

Because of its sexual content, the nineteenth-century printer of the records excised the Lecherous Swineherd. This account is taken from the original manuscript in the Connecticut State Archives.

William Payne appeared before the court to complain about Frost's "sinful miscarriages" toward his children and some others. Frost had previously been examined by the New Haven magistrates on September 8, 1662, and had been committed to prison and bound over for his appearance before the court. William now asked his son, John Payne, to speak to the court.

John Payne told the court that he desired to speak the truth concerning Frost. He and Frost were keeping sows together on a Sabbath Day in September.[2] When they came to the farther end of the meadow, they sat down to eat their dinners. Later, they made their way homeward, but after sundown, they sat down on a hill under a tree.

Frost pulled down his breeches and called to Payne, "Come John, let us play with our things together." Payne said no. Afterward, Frost shouted and called, "You whip me, and I will whip you." He made Payne pull down his trousers. They then whipped one other with some ferns.

Frost, being told to answer to this, told the court that they did not go to the upper end of the meadow on that day, and he denied all base sinful faults laid against him.

The court responded that he had acknowledged all of these passages in a previous examination, including these filthy actions. It warned Frost to take heed that "he did not add to his guilt by denials."

Goodwife Payne then related how her son told her of this "as a bad thing." It had troubled him, but he desired that she would not tell his father.

The court asked Goodwife Payne when John had told her this. She answered that it was at the beginning of the harvest.

John Payne was asked why he had not spoken of the matter before. He replied that he was afraid for he thought they would not believe him.

Mercy Payne was then called to tell what she had to say concerning Frost. When she was about to speak, however, the court saw fit to read what she had said in a previous examination.

In her examination, Mercy related that the first thing Frost did was to give her a ribbon. After this, one night, coming home, they were missing a sow. Her father was at the gate. Frost came and told her to go look for the sow. He would go with her, but her father would not. She went with Frost as far as a great log in the brook. He told her to sit down, but she would not. Then he took hold of her "and would do her," but she pulled away from him. He took hold of her again and tried to put his hand under her skirt. He said he would not hurt her, but she would not let him. She ran home as fast as she could, for she was frightened. Her mother being already in bed, Mercy said nothing to her that night.

The next day, another girl, Mary Curtis, saw Frost and Frank Bishop going into a rural area looking for their sows. Frost was a base rogue, for Mary was carrying a bottle of beer to him. He asked Mary to sit down and cocked his head, but she refused. Frost told Mary that Sarah Cooper had offered to do it with him. He put his hand under Mary's apron. Then she got up and ran home. She told her mother but was grievously frightened.

Curtis told Mercy of another time when she was working together with Frost. Frost wanted Mary to sit down almost every time, telling her that she was weary. She did not want to do so and asked why she should be weary. They then sat down. He went to put his hand under her apron as before, but she rose up and went to work. Mercy Payne told Curtis what Frost would have done to her. Then her mother called her away.

Mercy further said that Frost would not speak to her all winter after, but afterward he came to her house. He sat in the new room and started talking about a wife. He told Mercy he would have one as she, but she told him that she was not half old enough. Frost replied that she was old enough.

The next time Mercy saw Frost, it was a Saturday, after he had come to their house to spread dung. She carried him some beer, and he wanted her to stay to help him, and she did. He asked her again to be his wife and said she must make him a good wife. She told him she was not old enough and he had a great deal of time left in his service. Frost replied that he hoped he should obtain a little work. He would stay two years yet if she would have him. She asked what she would do if her father and mother were not willing. He answered that they would do well enough with the old folks if she would go with him. Mercy told Frost that she must go home because her mother would be angry. He told her that he would not displease her mother for she might come to be *his* mother. She then went home.

Frost stayed in the field, but when her father told Mercy to call him to dinner, she did. Frost asked her if her mother was angry. She said no. Then he asked her father and mother to let her go with him in the afternoon. They allowed her to do so.

Frost told her again that she must make a good wife, for he knew two in England who did so. He wanted to marry her, but Mercy would not. He asked her if she would not like him as much as another man. She said that she did. But why, then, would she not make him a good wife? She replied that she was too young. He asked how old was Sarah Cooper? He would stay until Mercy was as old as Sarah. Mercy told Frost she did not care to marry. She would stay until she was older. Frost asked Mercy if she did not go out on Sabbath Day nights. She told him no, her father did not allow it. She would not go out with him. She further told him that he wanted her to sit down with him many times a day, but she would not.

A "pretty while" after this, Mercy's father spoke to Frost to spread some more dung. Frost said he would, but his work was faulty. Then her father got him to help them plow half a day, but they presently broke the plow. John Payne went home, but Frost came to Mercy as she was spreading dung. Frost told her that he would help her that night and then they could sit down together. She said that he could, but she would work. But he persuaded her, and she sat down with him. Then Frost told her, "Come, let us see if we be fit to marry together." She replied, "No, John, then I should be a whore." He said, no, she would not; she would be a wife. She said, "Then I shall be hanged." He responded that she would never be hanged or whipped. But "what if they be whipped? That was nothing." Then she said it was a grievous sin. He said, no, everyone does so and must do so before they are married. She would not believe it. He insisted that they do. She said no, it's a grievous sin.

Later, Frost again implored Mercy to do have sex with him, but she said not if anyone should see them. He said no, they would not. She said that someone above could see them, but he said, "Come, let us." He wanted to know whether she would sleep with him or not. If anyone could see them, he would have already been to the court and fined a great deal, for he was a well-known offender in the town. Frost "did lie with her and had the use of her body at that time."

After this, Frost asked her to go out some nights. She told him no, she would not. Then he said that if any of their sows were wandering, tell him and he would go out with her to seek them. The next time Mercy saw Frost, she was at a cottage hoeing, and he was coming by with his hogs to drive them to market. He came after her to the bridge and then asked her to have sex with him again. She told him that she heard of calves being given water in the market and would go see if they were not theirs. Frost said she should have sex with him. She said no, what if anyone should see us? It was a grievous sin. He insisted, but she said she must go home. Did he think she must do whatever he wanted? But Frost told her she should go with him. As they were going home, "he had the use of her body again in a sinful way." This was after the planting season.

After this, Mercy and Frost were again working in the same lot. She was going to their spring to drink, and Frost followed her. He had her go to the bridge to look. But before they came to the spring he told her, "Come, let us lie together." He told her that she should go in the bushes in their lot near the spring. He did "lie with her and have the use of her body." He told her that he would give her whatever she wanted and talked of many things.

Another time, one Sabbath Day when Mercy was looking for a sow of hers that was lost, Frost was with her and offered to act in the same way again, but she would not. After this, when she was going to begin work, Frost met her in the corn. She was frightened to see him. He tried to have sex with her again, but she got away from him.

Mercy was asked "if she owned that which was said." She answered yes.

The court now turned to Frost. Frost owned all the times that he had been with Mercy but "denied those sinful actings with her." (He had given a sworn denial in a previous examination.) He granted, however, that "he had made love to her" and that once he had put his hand under her apron.

The court asked Frost whether he had attained any further realization of his sin in order to acknowledge it.

Frost responded that he would not consider it any further "if it was his last words he should speak."

The court advised him not to speak of last words for they are words of dishonor. God would bring them forth to light one day though he denied it.

Frost answered that he knew he must own it one day if it was true, if not now.

The court asked Frost how he could think that the boy John Payne could be lying. The daughter had given a long account. What temptation could there be to lie to their own shame?

Frost answered that he could not know the reason, but when he had been examined, he had been a witness against their father in the business for which he was confined.

The court noted that other witnesses had spoken similarly and that Frost had generally accepted all of these accounts. In addition, Frost had formerly been found guilty of the things that John charged him with and was punished for them. The court then asked to what end he had given Mercy the ribbons.

Frost answered that she had wanted a pair of those things. He had a blue ribbon that he sold her. She could have it for sixpence, but she couldn't afford it and so returned it to him.

Mercy denied that she was to give Frost anything for the ribbon. He gave it to her, but her mother, understanding what had happened, made her return it to him.

The court told Frost to seriously consider this and to understand his guilt.

Frost replied that, as he stood before them, so he must stand before God. He would wrong himself if he denied the truth. But if he admitted to something he didn't do, he would wrong himself.

Mercy further said that Frost wanted her go with him back to Jonathan Tuttle's barn as she was driving their sows, but he denied this.

The deputy governor informed the court that they had desired some Guilford women to "search" Mercy, and having done it, they all agreed she was "defiled."

The court asked Mercy if she "had any to do with any other in that way?" She answered no.

The court asked the same to Frost, and he answered, "No, no with her either." The court told Frost that it had cause to doubt his answer and that he had been untruthful by continuing his denials. Having considered the matter, the court noted that Frost had admitted he had made love to Mercy without the knowledge and consent of her parents. It ordered that he be corporally punished by whipping. In addition, "for his inveiglements by gift," it ordered that he pay a fine of forty shillings to the jurisdiction.

As for Mercy Payne, the court ordered that "she also be corporally punished by whipping, for her sinful compliance with him in such wickedness."

And as for John Payne, the court ordered that "he be whipped in the family" (i.e., his punishment was left up to his parents to impose).

William Payne pleaded that his daughter "had some weakness upon her," which had arisen since the women had examined her. He asked that her punishment might be forborne and replaced with a fine.

The court continued the case to the following morning to consider Payne's request. It then revoked the sentence it had previously imposed on Mercy and replaced it with a fine of fifty shillings payable to the jurisdiction.

⁂

The manuscript report of the Lecherous Swineherd omits a detail that almost any modern reader would want to know. How old were John and Mercy Payne? If they were adults, modern courts would be inclined to give all the actors involved a substantial degree of sexual autonomy. If they were children, Frost would more likely be viewed as a sexual predator, with the severity of his offense increasing as the age of the children decreased.

While William Payne described John and Mercy Payne as "children," the court did not think in terms of our modern notions of childhood. The ultimate sentence that John "be whipped in the family" does seem to make some concession to John's youth, but that is as far as the court was willing to bend. The initial sentence of corporal punishment by whipping imposed on Mercy Payne was the exact corporal punishment ordered for Frost, and the modified sentence of a fifty-shilling fine imposed on Mercy was a larger fine than the forty-shilling fine levied on Frost. Both Mercy and Frost were treated as adults.

The most logical conclusion from the record, however, is that John and Mercy were children. The fact that John's punishment was left to the family suggests that he was a preadolescent child. Mercy appears to have been older than John, but she remained in the care of her parents and told Frost that she "was not half old enough" to be his wife. Frost's reply that she was "old enough" suggests she might have been an adolescent, but that is as close as we can come.

Frost merited our sympathy for the vicious punishment he received in the Farmhand Arsonist, but given his subsequent behavior, sympathy for him becomes more difficult to generate. He was fourteen years old at the time of the 1656 incident, so he must have been about twenty in 1662. Although the court never mentioned his earlier arson conviction, it noted that he had previously been found guilty of acts like those John had charged him with and was punished for those offenses. Frost had attempted to seduce young girls other than Mercy Payne as well. (Mercy describes his dealings with Mary Curtis, and Frost implies he has been intimate with Sarah Cooper.) He assured Mercy that no one had seen them together because, if they *had* been seen, he would surely have been taken to court, given his well-known-offender status. He was, in modern parlance, a "person well known to the authorities."

If John and Mercy were indeed children, Frost unquestionably deserved punishment. The great irony of the case, however, is that the punishment selected by the court—whipping—was exactly the punishment Frost wished to receive. It appears that the corporal punishment levied on Frost in 1656 had not had the desired deterrent effect. To the contrary, Frost *wanted* to be whipped. He had actively solicited John to engage in a mutual whipping game. He subsequently told Mercy that whipping was "nothing." The court seemed to be entirely unaware of the utter inutility of the punishment it pronounced.

The result of this sad case is unknowable. The New Haven Colony would shortly cease to exist, and we never hear of John Frost again.

33

❦❦❦

THE

BURNING

BARN

❦❦❦

The last recorded trial in the New Haven Colony occurred before the Court of Magistrates on December 9, 1663.[1] Sadly, this final judicial act would demonstrate that the court's harsh treatment of children had not lessened over the course of time.

John Cooper, a deputy from New Haven, complained to the court that Mary Betts, a girl who lived with him, "had fired [burned] his barn and corn in it." He further alleged that Mary's sister, Hannah Betts, and the girls' mother (whom we know only as "Goodwife Betts") were accessories in the crime. Goodwife Betts was present, but the court wished her "to depart the court for a while."[2]

Mary was called and asked her name. When she "owned" that she was indeed Mary Betts, the court read a transcript of a prior examination taken before the magistrates in New Haven on November 25, 1663.

During this pretrial examination, the deputy governor (DG), James Bishop of New Haven, speaking for the court, called Mary. A lengthy dialogue ensued.

DG: We heard that you kindled the fire in your master's barn, whereby the barn and the corn was all consumed. How did you do it?

MARY: I did it with a firestick, which I took out of the house.

DG: How long were you about it?

MARY: A pretty while.

DG: What moved you to it?

MARY: My sister, Hannah, bid me when I was at their house.

DG: What did your sister say to you?

MARY: She said that if she was bound there, she would set the house and barn afire too.

DG: Did you dislike your place?

MARY: I loved my dame well, but I had rather go home to see my mother than stay there. I wished I might go home with my sister. My sister advised me to do it, for my sister was vexed with my dame because my dame chided me. She chided me because I could not do the work in the house, such as sweeping the house and washing the dishes.

DG: What did your dame say?

MARY: I had not had it in my thought to do it before my sister spoke so to me.

DG: What moved you to do it yesterday? Did your dame chide you?

MARY: Yes.

DG: For what?

MARY: I took some of her apples out of the tub. My dame said she would fill the tub again, and if I took any more she would whip me.

DG: Where did your sister give you that counsel?

MARY: It was in the yard, when my dame was not at home.

She said to me that she could not abide to live there, for she
would be nothing but chided.

DG: We have heard that you have threatened since to burn the
house. Why did you say so?

MARY: Because they vexed me. I spoke this to John Ginne and
Goodwife Dickerman.

DG: Do you not know it to be a wicked thing that you have
done?

MARY: Yes.

The examination having been read, Mary "owned it in all the
particulars." She also told the court that what she had said concerning her sister was true. A new examination of Mary ensued.

COURT: Have you considered your wickedness??

MARY: I will not do so again.

COURT: We understand that your mother was with you at the
marshal's.[3] What did she say to you?

MARY: She bid me to speak the truth.

COURT: Did you set the barn on fire?

MARY: Yes.

COURT: Who saw you?

MARY: Zachariah and Nathaniel Howe.

COURT: Did your sister, Hannah, bid you?

MARY: She did.

Goodwife Betts: Her sister did not bid her. Mary is a lying girl,
but Hannah would not lie.[4]

COURT (to Mary): You have done evil both against God and
your master. You have done the Devil's work and given an
ill example to others. Therefore, you need to crave mercy so

far as may stand with justice. Did your sister not tell you of
another person who acted so?

MARY: She told me that Mr. Crane's maid burnt a barn and had
nothing done to her and was released from her service. If she
did it she would have nothing done to her but be chided. I
told my sister I would not do it, but she told me I should and
then I should go home. She would have me go home with
her. She said if she was there she should burn the house and
barn too.

The court now called Hannah.

COURT: You have heard what your sister has charged. Consider
in whose presence you are, not only before authority but
in the presence of God, who will be a swift witness against
those that shall speak falsely and judge over all your
witnessing. Therefore look that you speak the truth.

HANNAH: I hope I should.

COURT: Were you not at Goodman Cooper's a little while
before the fire?

HANNAH: I was there, but how long before, I know not. I went
away the last day of the week, which was seven nights before
the fire. I had absented myself without leave. When I could
not get over the ferry, I came not to my master's house but
lay about from place to place all the Sabbath until I went
away to my mother.

COURT: What do you have to say to what your sister has
charged you, of counseling her to burn your master's barn?

HANNAH: I deny it. She must lay it upon somebody.

COURT: Why upon you?

HANNAH: I am a child, and it was better to lay it upon me than
anyone else.

COURT: What about the story of Mr. Crane's maid?

HANNAH: I did not tell her that story. I had not so little wit as to think Mary should not be punished if she did so.

Goodwife Betts (GB) was now called.

COURT: We have a sad occasion to call you concerning your children. We desire that truth might appear so that God might be glorified.

GB: I desire it with all my heart.

COURT: We desire that you join with us to find out the truth.

GB: She did it.

The court turned to Mary, who was now in the presence of her mother.

COURT: What moved you to burn your master's barn?

MARY: My sister, Hannah.

Returning to Goodwife Betts, the court continued.

COURT: It was unnatural for Mary to do thus if it was not so. There was no necessity of her laying this upon Hannah or anyone else. It was beyond the device of such a child to frame such a story as she has always stood to, having been charged to speak the truth. What have you to say to it?

GB: I hope it was not in her sister to do any such thing. I spoke with Mary today, and she told me that she had said she did it, but she did not do it.

And then the court returns to Mary.

COURT: Did you tell your mother that you did not burn the barn?

MARY: No.

And the court goes back to Goodwife Betts.

COURT: You defamed authority when you were at Branford.

GB: I deny it. Indeed, I had something boiling in my mind against someone about this business. I told a friend, who counseled me to be silent if I could not prove it. I am sorry that I should have any such thoughts.

COURT: Take notice how God has brought your own daughter to confront you and her sister before the Court.

GB: My conscience is clear in it. It was the manner of my daughter, Mary, that when she was at fault at home, she would lay it on her sister.

The court goes back to Hannah.

COURT: Mind what your sister has charged you with. What yet have you to say to it?

HANNAH: There is nothing of it true.

Magistrate Jasper Crane speaks.[5]

CRANE: Hannah stood before us at Branford. When we told her she was a bold, malapert [saucy] girl, her mother said she was glad she was so, for the righteous is as bold as a lion.

The court goes back to Goodwife Betts.

COURT: Did you say so?

GB: I might have said so.

(The court "sharply reproved" Goodwife Betts for this statement.)

John Cooper speaks.

COOPER: I have heard that Goodwife Betts, being at Goodwife
Jones's house, hearing of the fire but not of who had done it,
said that she looked on it as a good providence that she had
no private discourse with her daughter Mary the fourth day
of the week before the fire, she being in New Haven that day.

And the court returns to Goodwife Betts.

COURT: Why did you thus speak if you did not think it was
your daughter?
GB: I had no cause, but they were speaking of my older girl.
Court: There was some falsity in your speech. You said that
Goodman Andrews was the first man that saw the fire,
and it was so high that the child could not do it. Goodman
Andrews was then at the farm and never saw it. You stood
in the defense of your elder daughter, in whose speeches
falsities appeared. You were against your younger daughter,
against which no such thing yet appears.

John Cooper speaks again.

COOPER: Hannah Betts spoke falsely. She said she rode from
Branford to the New Haven ferry, and from the ferry to Mr.
Trowbridge's, when there was evident proof that she did not
ride from the farm to the waterside.
COURT (following an adjournment): What do you think your
loss might be?
COOPER: I would give one hundred pounds to be set in the
same state as I was before, but I desire that what is done is
that all might hear and fear and do no more so wickedly.

The governor, Lieutenant John Nash of New Haven, speaks.

GOVERNOR: I have not much further to say to the little girl, but the great girl is left under such suspicion, her sister having laid such an accusation against her, even beyond her own capacity.

The court returns to Hannah.

COURT: What do you have to say further? Are you guilty of no?
HANNAH: No.
COURT: Did you not tell her that story about Mr. Crane's maid burning a barn?
HANNAH: I spoke to her of that, but in no way such as charged. Maybe I said Mr. Crane's maid did burn a barn and was whipped for it, but I know not on what occasion I spoke it. It was at Goodman Dickerman's.

Mary speaks.

MARY: She never spoke to me before that time in the yard when my dame was from home.

The court goes back to Hannah.

COURT: You contradicted yourself, before denying it, but now granting it, yet mincing it as if it was in that place or to that purpose. If you would bring out the whole truth in a sensible way, there might be hope for you. Otherwise, what advantage would it be to you to bring part of the truth and mix lies with it?
(No answer is recorded.)

The court, "having spent much time to find out the truth in the case," proceeded to sentence the defendants. The court turned first to Mary. It declared that she was convicted upon due examination in open court by her own confession and other circumstances that she willfully "and in a degree maliciously" set fire to and burned Cooper's barn and corn on November 24, 1663, to the endangerment of his dwelling house and other buildings.

Mary was sentenced to be publicly whipped. At the same time, she was to wear a halter visibly about her neck. The court explained that the crime she had perpetrated was capital by the law, "deserving death were she of age capable of such censure." The sentence was "to be executed in terror to others to prevent the like wicked practice by her or any other for the future."

Additionally, to satisfy Cooper for the great damage he sustained by the fire, the court ordered that "he may at his liberty sell or dispose the said Mary as a bond servant, for and toward his satisfaction, to any person and into any place within some or other of the English plantations of any of the four united colonies in New England and not elsewhere,[6] that she may live under public ordinances for her soul's good."

The court now turned to Hannah. It declared that Mary had accused her in open court of having counseled and abetted her "in the said wicked act." Although by all circumstances duly weighed, she seemed to the court to be guilty, "yet wanting due proof," the court could not proceed to censure her in this case. However, other complaints had also come in against Hannah, and proof had been made "of her contemptuous carriage before authority, her frequent lying, and sundry disorders on the Lord's Day and other times."

For all this, the court ordered Hannah to be set in the stocks for one hour. This was to be imposed at the time of the execution of the sentence previously imposed upon Mary.

For extra measure, the court ordered that the respective sentences imposed on Mary and Hannah would each be imposed *twice*. The first time would be in New Haven. The second time would be in Branford, "for a terror there if the said Mary shall go thither to dwell."

The court finally turned to Goodwife Betts. It pronounced that she "appeared faulty in respect of divers [various] untruths, contemptuous carriage before authority at Branford, evil example to her children, tending to harden them in their evil ways, contrary to the duty of her relation and to the good behavior she stands bound to by the court or the authority of Branford." The court consequently ordered "further examination of the premises," after which it could "proceed against her according to law."

Quietly proud of the last sentences it would ever impose, the court receded into the mists of history.

The court ended its history on an appalling note. Mary Betts was, in the words of the governor, a "little girl." The thought that a judicial tribunal could deliberately order a little girl to be publically whipped on two different occasions in two different towns, wear a halter around her neck, and be sold into virtual slavery chills the modern soul. The fact that the court ostensibly wished to protect the "good" of Mary's own soul makes its final judicial act even more chilling.

The facts of this case are reminiscent of two other arson cases we have seen: the Farmhand Arsonist and the Milford Arson

Case. In each of those cases, as in this, a child working as a servant started a fire and destroyed a building along with much valuable property. In each of those cases, as in this, the child was ordered whipped and placed into lengthy servitude. But the facts of this case are even more pathetic. John Frost was fourteen years old at the time of the Farmhand Arsonist, and Jacobus Loper was twelve at the time of the Milford Arson Case. We don't know how old Mary Betts was, but she appears to have been a small child. She was too young to do the sweeping and dishwashing she was ordered to do. She was threatened with whipping for taking a few apples. She wanted to go home to her mother and sister, from whom she was separated. Her mother, who publicly denounced her to the court as a liar, seems to have rejected her in favor of her older sister. In ordering this small child to be punished as it did, the court closed out its existence by reaching new depths of callousness and brutality.

❦

ACKNOWLEDGMENTS

❦

My scholarly debts go back decades to two inspirational Carleton College professors, Carl Weiner and Phil Niles, who gave me a love of history that has never quite departed. More recently, Akhil Amar has generously encouraged my legal scholarship.

This book would not have been possible were it not for the work of Charles J. Hoadly, who, in his capacity as Connecticut state librarian in the 1850s, supervised the transcription and publication of most (but, as explained in the introduction, "The New Haven Trials," not quite all) of the manuscript records of the New Haven Colony. Mark Jones, the Connecticut state archivist, graciously provided photocopies of hitherto untranscribed manuscript pages.

Jon Butler, Walter Woodward, and Gene Fidell provided helpful comments on some early chapters. Two anonymous readers read the book in its entirety and contributed additional suggestions.

Parker Smathers has edited the book with great skill and unflagging enthusiasm. I have been blessed to have him as an editor.

My greatest debt, by far, is to Jean Blue, who has encouraged this project from the start and has read every word with a critical eye. Her impressive skill in helping me to decipher the seventeenth-century manuscript records of the New Haven Colony has doubtless been honed by four decades of experience in reading my even more inscrutable handwriting. Since she has been a central part of my entire adult life, I owe her much more than the dedication of this book. But that, at least, is a start.

∞∞∞∞

NOTES

∞∞∞∞

*The following abbreviations have been
used throughout the notes.*

Blackstone: William Blackstone, Commentaries on the Laws of England
(1765–69)

CM: Court of Magistrates

GC: General Court

MS: Manuscript Records of the Colony of New Haven (Connecticut
State Archives, Hartford, Connecticut)

OED: Oxford English Dictionary (1933)

1R: Charles J. Hoadly, Records of the Colony and Plantation
of New Haven from 1638 to 1649 (1857).

2R: Charles J. Hoadly, Records of the Colony or Jurisdiction
of New Haven from May, 1653, to the Union (1858)

Quotations from the Bible are from the King James Version (1611).

INTRODUCTION: THE NEW HAVEN TRIALS

1. Compare, for example, the contemporaneous reports of judicial
proceedings in the neighboring Connecticut Colony. A representative
notation reads, "Matthew Allen plaintiff against John Coggen defendant,
in an action of slander, to the damage of a thousand pounds. The jury
finds for the plaintiff damages 20 pounds." 1 Public Records of the
Colony of Connecticut 66 (1850) (proceedings of September 2, 1641).

2. Thus, Thomas Fugill, in "New Haven's Watergate" (chapter 5), confronted with inconvenient evidence, "began to turn and wind, so as to evade the Governor's testimony." Charles J. Hoadly, Records of the Colony and Plantation of New Haven from 1638 to 1649 (1857) (hereafter "1R"), at 224.

3. The records from 1644 to 1653 disappeared in the mid-eighteenth century. 1R iv.

4. 13 Public Records of the Colony of Connecticut 580–81 (1885).

5. 1R v.

6. 1R ii.

7. Charles J. Hoadly, Records of the Colony or Jurisdiction of New Haven from May, 1653, to the Union (1858) (hereafter "2R").

8. 2R 137.

9. This last problem has been partially ameliorated by the recent practice of scanning books no longer subject to copyright protection and selling inexpensive reprints on the Internet. Excellent reproductions of 1R and 2R have been made available by the Cornell University Library Digital Collections.

10. Helpful summaries of the colony's history can be found in Isabel MacBeath Calder, The New Haven Colony (1934), and the opening chapters of Rollin G. Osterweis, Three Centuries of New Haven, 1638–1938 (1953).

11. 3 Dictionary of American Biography 612 (1931).

12. Osterweis, *supra* note 10, at 7.

13. 1R 11. The site of this meeting appears to be that of Yale's present-day Silliman College.

14. 1R 12. (Modernized spelling is used throughout this introduction.)

15. 1R 17.

16. 1R 20. The seven "foundational" members were Theophilus Eaton, John Davenport, Robert Newman, Matthew Gilbert, Thomas Fugill, John Ponderson, and Jeremy Dixon.

17. The word "court" should not be taken in its modern sense. It refers to an assembly of the qualified members of the company. 2 Oxford English Dictionary (1933) (hereafter "OED"), at 1091.

18. 1R 20.

19. 1R 20–21.

20. Osterweis, *supra* note 10, at 26.

21. The New Haven Colony's territory was noncontiguous, being divided by the town of Fairfield, then part of the Connecticut Colony. This somewhat odd territorial configuration reflects the fact that transportation by water was, at the time, more efficient than travel by land.

22. 1R 112.

23. 1R 112–15.

24. *See* The Federalist No. 47 (James Madison, 1788).

25. 1R 191.

26. 2R 146–47.

27. The 1648 Massachusetts Code is officially titled "The Book of the General Laws and Liberties Concerning the Inhabitants of the Massachusetts." It was published in Cambridge in 1648. The sole existing copy of that work is in the Henry E. Huntington Library, which published a reproduction in 1929.

28. 1 Public Records of the Colony of Connecticut 509 (1850).

29. 2R 154.

30. The 1656 Laws are officially entitled "New-Haven's Settling in New-England and Some Laws for Government: Published for the Use of that Colony."

31. 2R 571–72.

32. 2R 186.

33. "The grant to Connecticut was probably made without thought of the consequences to the New Haven Colony. There is not a scrap of evidence that the king intended to abolish the colony on the Sound to punish it for sheltering Edward Whalley and William Goffe, the regicides." Calder, *supra*, note 10, at 230 note 46.

34. Osterweis, *supra* note 10, at 61.

35. 2R 553.

36. 2R 555.

37. 1R 114.

38. The 1643 fundamental order provided that each town could elect a "magistrate or magistrates." 1R 113.

39. 2R 168–69.

40. 1R 115.

41. 1R 116.

42. 1R 115.

43. 1R 11 note *.

44. 2R 327.

45. 1R 113.

46. 2R 26.

47. Calder, *supra* note 10, at 125. "Many colonial charters expressly preserved trial by jury." John H. Langbein, Renee Letow Lerner & Bruce P. Smith, History of the Common Law 475 (2009). For the Massachusetts Colony, *see* The 1648 Massachusetts Code, *supra* note 27, at 1. For the Connecticut Colony, *see* the 1650 Code of Laws, *supra* note 1, at 535.

48. 1R 112.

49. Calder, *supra* note 10, at 125–26.

50. 1R 115.

51. Ensign Alexander Bryan makes several appearances as an attorney in 2R.

52. Although the questioning procedure of the New Haven Colony courts finds no close parallel in the English-speaking world, it strikingly resembled that of a Chinese court I observed in 1995. In the course of a civil trial in the Chengdu Intermediate People's Court, the chief judge of a three-judge panel ignored the lawyers for the respective parties and directly questioned the parties themselves in a back-and-forth manner quite like that of the New Haven courts of long ago. By doing so, the court was able to ascertain the facts of the case in about forty-five minutes. A similar hearing in an American court would probably have taken at least a day. Jon C. Blue, *Efficiency Is the Rule in Chinese Court*, 21 Conn. L. Trib. No. 28, at 25 (July 10, 1995).

53. Perhaps for this reason, there is no discernable jurisprudential distinction between the General Court and the Court of Magistrates.

54. *California v. Green*, 399 U.S. 149, 157 n. 10 (1970).

55. F. W. Maitland, 1 Year Books of Edward II ix (vol. 17, Selden Society, 1903).

56. *Id.*, at xx.

1. THE INDIAN'S NAME

1. 1R 22–24. (General Court [hereafter "GC"], 1639). All quotations from the trial that are used in this chapter are taken from this case record. This is the case for every initial note for each chapter.

2. Some of the more sanguinary aspects of the war are explored in Andrew Lipman, *"A meanes to knitt them togeather": The Exchange of Body Parts in the Pequot War*, LXV Wm & Mary Q, No. 1 (January 2008).

3. A mantle-tree was a beam across the top of a fireplace supporting the mantle. 6 OED 138.

2. THE PIGLET'S PATERNITY

1. 1R 62–69, 72–73 (GC, 1642).

2. "If a man lie with a beast, he shall surely be put to death: and ye shall slay the beast."

3. John Winthrop, 2 History of New England 61 (1826).

4. The records state that the General Court met on "the 6th of the 2d Month, 1642." This cannot mean February 6, 1642, since the magistrates were not informed of the existence of the deformed piglet until February 14. Keeping in mind that, prior to 1751, the English legal year began on March 25, the records' reference to "the 2d Month" must be a reference to April rather than February. This conclusion is buttressed by Spencer's later acknowledgment in his gallows speech that his execution had been respited for a period of five or six weeks. But the specific date of the General Court's decision does not appear to be April 6. At the end of the session, Spencer was ordered executed "on the 6th day next, being the 8 of April." This order must have been given on or about April 2. There are two possible explanations here. One is simply that the dates in the

records are hopelessly confused. The second, more forgiving, explanation is that the recordkeeper began counting the days on March 25, the beginning of the legal year, and that the records' reference to "the 6th of the 2d Month" (1R 69) is to a session (which considered other business before it got to Spencer) that *began* on March 30, 1642.

5. David H. Flaherty, Privacy in Colonial New England 240 (1972).

3. THE EXPLODING GUN

1. 1R 176–78 (GC, 1645).

2. Calculating the present value of centuries-old monetary awards necessarily involves a great deal of guesswork, especially since market transactions in the New Haven Colony tended to involve barter rather than monetary payments. The value of the twenty-pound award given to Medcalfe is hinted at by a separate dispute heard by the General Court the same day involving an agreement by unrelated parties to trade two cows for twelve pounds' worth of cloth. By this calculus, one cow was worth six pounds, and a twenty-pound award was worth a little more than three cows.

3. A "bezar-stone" (bezoar) was a stone made from the intestinal calcification of a Middle Eastern animal, thought in those days to be useful in warding off plagues and poisons.

4. *Chandelor v. Lopus*, 79 E.R. 3 (Exch. 1603).

4. THE "BILLINGSGATE SLUT"

1. 1R 180–81 (GC, 1645).

2. Billingsgate was a ward in London known for its fish market and the foul language associated with it. 1 OED 863.

3. "Froward" is a now-obsolete adjective meaning "difficult to deal with." 4 OED 571.

4. A cucking stool was an instrument of punishment for scolds consisting of a chair (sometimes in the form of a commode) in which the offender was fastened and exposed to the jeers of bystanders. 2 OED 1235.

5. R. H. Helmholz, Select Cases on Defamation to 1600 xv (vol. 101, Selden Society, 1985).

6. Thus in *Holwood v. Hopkins* (C.P. 1600), an action for the words "thy mistress is an arrant whore and would have lain with me seven years ago" was held to be "spiritual" in nature and dismissed by the Court of Common Pleas. *Id.*, at 89.

5. NEW HAVEN'S WATERGATE

1. 1R 221–25, 262–64 (GC, 1646).

6. THE SEXUAL HARASSMENT CASE

1. 1R 233–39 (GC, 1646).

2. The record states that Robinson "put his hand under her coates." The term "coates" does not refer to an outer garment worn on the upper body, as in modern usage, but to a skirt or petticoat. I have, I hope accurately, translated the term as "skirt." Modern undergarments are an invention of the nineteenth century. Descriptions of sexual activity contained in the New Haven Colony records suggest that persons of neither gender wore undergarments at the time. The wording of the text is reminiscent of a well-known passage in *The Diary of Samuel Pepys*, describing his wife's discovery of him with a member of the household staff: "My wife, coming up suddenly, did find me embracing the girl con my hand sub su coats." Robert Latham & William Matthews, 9 The Diary of Samuel Pepys 337 (1976) (October 25, 1668).

3. The New Haven Colony records show that Goodwife Fancy was convicted of the theft of several household items in 1643 and was sentenced to "be severely whipped." She had previously been whipped twice in the Connecticut Colony for similar crimes.

4. On August 4, 1646, one Thomas Robinson was accused of stealing over sixteen pounds of nails from a ship. We don't know if this was the same Thomas Robinson, but in any event the records do not indicate that the defendant in that case appeared in court to answer the charge.

7. THE WOMEN DISSIDENTS

1. 1R 242–57 (GC, 1646).

2. The records identify each woman only as "Mrs." Mrs. Brewster appears as "Lucy Brewster" elsewhere in the records. The first names of Mrs. Moore and Mrs. Leach nowhere appear. We are, however, informed that Mrs. Leach was the daughter of Mrs. Moore.

3. Mrs. Eaton was the second wife of Governor Theophilus Eaton. We don't know her first name either.

4. "For the perfecting of the saints, for the work of the ministry, for the edifying of the body of Christ."

5. Mrs. Eaton did not believe in infant baptism and departed from the church whenever baptism was administered. She would additionally absent herself from John Davenport's sermons when she felt inclined to do so. For these and other "miscarriages," she was cast out of the church in March 1645. Leonard Bacon, *Thirteen Historical Discourses* 296–306 (1839).

6. See *id.*

7. "And he gave some, apostles; and some, prophets; and some, evangelists; and some, pastors and teachers."

8. THE SHIPWRECK

1. 1R 281–91 (GC, 1647).

2. A shallop is "a large, heavy boat fitted with one or more masts and carrying fore-and-aft or lug sails." 9 OED 614.

9. THE FAULTY SHOES

1. 1R 345–53 (GC, 1647).

2. Gregory's numbers make no sense, since the price would be a wash, and Gregory's labor in making the shoes would have been done for nothing.

3. In shoemaking terminology, a rand is "a strip of leather placed under the quarters of a boot or shoe, to make this level before the lifts of the

heel are attached." 8 OED 137. A welt is "a strip of leather placed between and sewn to the edge of the sole and the turned-in edge of the upper in soling a boot or shoe." 12 OED 310.

4. *Munn v. Illinois*, 94 U.S. 113, 126 (1877).

5. Carl Kaysen, *In Memoriam: Charles E. Wyzanski, Jr.*, 100 Harv. L. Rev. 713, 714 (1987).

6. *United Shoe Machinery Corp. v. United States*, 347 U.S. 521 (1954).

10. THE DRUNKEN SAILORS

1. 1R 393–96 (GC, 1648).

2. The record is confusing, but it appears that the crews of three different ships were involved in the brawl—the *Susan*, "the ship here built," and "a pinnace lately come in from Boston." The crew of the "pinnace" apparently avoided arrest. The crews of the *Susan* and "the ship here built" were brought before the court along with Bassett, the alleged provider of alcohol.

3. A *pottle* is "a measure of capacity for liquids . . . equal to two quarts of half a gallon." 7 OED 1195.

4. 1R 218.

5. *United States v. Kirby*, 74 U.S. (7 Wall.) 482, 486–87 (1869).

11. THE COMPETING CLAIMANTS

1. 1R 467–69 (GC, 1649).

2. Cotton wool is "cotton in its raw and wooly state, gathered from the bolls of the plant." 2 OED 1046.

3. A thorough substantive analysis would be a bit more complicated than the summary in the text. An obvious response to Evance's substantive claim would be that his contract was with Peirse, not Westerhousen, and if he wanted to get paid on the contract, he should sue Peirse, not Westerhousen. That response might be dispositive in an ordinary contract case. But Evance claimed that the contract with Peirse gave him a security interest in the ship. If this was the case, Evance would be able to assert a

legal ownership interest in the ship if Peirse didn't pay him. Since we don't know what the contract actually said, this claim is impossible to analyze. Both modern and seventeenth-century rules of admiralty law would add another level of complexity involving the law of claims made upon ships. The General Court did not, however, consider itself subject to admiralty rules. For present purposes, we'll simply take Evance at his word.

4. In practice, a treaty or controlling statute often exists. As a practical matter, judges have to take pains in international cases to be sure that they consider all of the applicable law.

5. This is called an *in rem* action, which is Latin for an action "against the thing." The idea is that the action is brought against the ship itself rather than against a person such as the owner. The phrase describes an important category of legal actions and has thus far proven resistant to modern efforts to reform the law by phrasing it in plain English.

6. *Williams v. George*, 11 U.S. (7 Cranch) 423 (1813).

12. THE FRISKY COUPLE

1. 1R 469–71 (GC, 1649).

2. Who was "Mr. Goodanhousen"? The records indicate that the reference is to Samuel Goodenhousen, who, like William Westerhousen, was a planter in the colony of Dutch origin. 1R 355. Although the record in the Frisky Couple refers to Goodenhousen as Rebecka Turner's "father," other records (as well as the implications of the case itself) suggest that he was her stepfather. 1R 480.

3. See *id.*

4. 1R 480.

13. THE RHODE ISLAND PRIVATEER

1. 2R 26–28 (CM, 1653).

2. The other members of the Court of Magistrates were Governor Eaton, Francis Newman, a magistrate for New Haven, and Captain John Atwood, a magistrate for Milford.

14. THE REPUTED WITCH

1. 2R 29–36 (CM, 1653).

2. The records contain no mention of any execution for witchcraft in the history of the colony.

3. "Matthew Hopkins," 28 Oxford Dictionary of National Biography 62 (2004).

4. William Blackstone, Commentaries on the Laws of England (vol. 4, 1765–69) 60 (hereafter Blackstone).

15. THE MILFORD BESTIALITY CASE

1. 2R 132–44; Manuscript Records of the Colony of New Haven 85–86 (Connecticut State Archives, Hartford, Connecticut [hereafter MS]) (CM, 1655).

2. The state archivist has generously provided me with photocopies of the relevant manuscripts.

16. THE BOAT SEX CASE

1. 2R 134–37 (CM, 1655).

2. Here, as elsewhere in the New Haven Colony records, "miscarriages" is an all-purpose word for offenses deemed criminal.

17. THE YOUTH SEX CASES

1. 2R 137–39 (CM, 1655).

2. The word used in the records is "coats." *See* chap. 6, note 2.

3. The word used in the records is "owned."

4. We don't know how old Knight, Coventry, and Tuttill were. It seems a fair guess, however, that they were all young people employed by Judson to work in a menial capacity on his farm. Tuttill seems to have been a contemporary of Clarke's. Knight may have been somewhat older, since we are told that he had a criminal record.

5. *Hayden v. Smithville Manufacturing Co.*, 29 Conn. 548, 558 (1861).

18. THE DISPUTED WILL

1. 2R 159–61 (CM, 1656).

2. Southold, on the North Fork of Long Island, was part of the New Haven Colony until 1662.

3. An overseer was "a person appointed by a testator to supervise or assist the executor or executors of the will." 7 OED 322.

4. The court is referring to the ancient right of dower. A husband could not (and cannot today) simply leave nothing to his surviving wife. The surviving wife had, at a minimum, a statutory share of a life estate of one-third of the property passing under the will. With updated gender references, this remains the law in Connecticut today. Conn. Gen. Stat. § 45a-436(a) (2015). So, if Hindes had left his widow nothing in his will, she could have gone to the New Haven court and received her statutory share.

5. The court is referencing Deuteronomy 21:17. According to this biblical passage, if a man has two wives, one of whom he dislikes, and both wives bear him sons, the first being born to the disliked wife, his will must give the firstborn "a double portion of all that he hath: for he is the beginning of his strength."

6. The court is paraphrasing 2 Corinthians 12:14. ("The children ought not to lay up for the parents, but the parents for the children.")

7. 2R 146–47.

8. The book is entitled *New-Haven's Settling in New-England and Some Lawes for Government: Published for the Use of That Colony* and was printed in London in 1656. The book is reprinted at 2R 559.

19. THE FARMHAND ARSONIST

1. 2R 169–71 (GC, 1656).

2. Wakeman sat as a member of the very tribunal that imposed Frost's sentence.

3. It appears by this that Frost had been imprisoned since his arrest.

4. Arson, including burning a barn or a haystack, was a capital crime

in English law. 4 Blackstone 220–21. The 1656 New Haven Laws did not specifically mention arson but had a catchall provision stating that capital cases, "where there is no express Law, shall be judged according to the word and Law of God, by the General Court." 2R 572. As we have seen, the New Haven court was capable of interpreting "the word and Law of God" as being very harsh indeed.

20. THE STOLEN SILVERWARE

1. 2R 187–89 (CM, 1656).

2. The exact date of Wood's trial is a matter of some speculation. The records state that it occurred on "the 5th of the 6th Month, 1656." While this could refer to June 5, 1656, in all likelihood it does not. As readers of Thomas Hardy novels will recall, the legal year at the time began on Lady Day, March 25. The "first month" of the legal year would be April, and the "sixth month" would be September.

3. Eaton had sat as a magistrate on the Boat Sex Case.

4. Larceny of an item above the value of twelve pence from a dwelling house was a capital offense in England. 4 Blackstone 240.

5. Deputy Governor Goodyear was a member of the court.

6. The text is ambiguous here. The text states that "they give him fourteen days time that he may take his opportunity to sell him in any of the other colonies or take other course for his security." Does "him" refer to Goodyear or to Wood? Conceivably, Wood was being given a chance to raise money himself by indenturing his own services. This seems doubtful, however, since the court next proceeded to order that Wood lie in prison in irons while remaining in the colony. Under these circumstances, the only person in a position to sell Wood or his services was Goodyear.

7. *Trop v. Dulles*, 356 U.S. 86, 102 (1958).

8. Compare the lenient punishment for theft of an animal with the draconian punishment for sexual contact with an animal. "Whosoever lieth with a beast shall surely be put to death" (Exodus 22:19).

9. 2R 575.

1. 2R 198–200 (CM, 1657).

2. The date is, once more, a guess. The records give the date as "25th 12th Mo. 1656." Assuming this is a reference to the legal year beginning March 25, 1656 (with first month of that year being April), the case was probably heard at the very end of the legal year, on March 25, 1657.

3. Technically, Tompson claimed the "estate" of John Roberts. "Estate" is something of an all-purpose legal word, referring to an interest in property. In modern parlance, it often refers to the property that a person leaves after death. In this case, where it was unclear whether Roberts was dead in the first place, Tompson was simply claiming property held by Wakeman on Roberts's behalf.

4. The records state that Thomas's document was dated "5th day 10th mon: 1656." The date in the text is a guess based on the chronology of the legal year.

5. The common-law rule is a product of the nineteenth century. *Nepean v. Doe dem. Knight*, 150 E.R. 1021, 1023 (Exch. 1837); *Davie v. Briggs*, 97 U.S. 628, 634–35 (1878). It was, however, based in part on an English bigamy statute enacted in 1603. 1 Jac. I, c. 11.

6. *Bacon v. Sanders*, 54 Pa. (4 Whart.) 148, 165 (1839).

7. The records are clear that Vicars had been Roberts's "espoused wife."

22. THE ATTEMPTED BESTIALITY CASE

1. 2R 223–24; MS 145–46 (CM, 1657).

2. The date is a guess. The records give the date of Ferris's trial as "30th 4th Mo, 1657." Assuming April to be the first full month of the legal year, a date of July 30, 1657, is appropriate.

3. This somewhat elliptical reference seems to describe a procedure in which Accerly had previously given his testimony—either oral or written—under oath. He did not repeat this testimony at the actual trial but instead "affirmed" it in the presence of the accused. The manuscript later mentions that Accerly had been examined at Stamford.

4. 2 F. Pollock & F. Maitland, History of English Law 508 n. 4 (2d ed. 1903).

5. Francis B. Sayre, *Criminal Attempts*, 41 Harv. L. Rev. 821, 829 (1928). The Star Chamber era was, however, at least possibly in the memory of the New Haven magistrates of the 1650s.

6. *See People v. Dlugash*, 363 N.E.2d 1155, 1159 (N.Y. 1977). *Dlugash* holds that it is possible to attempt to kill a man who (unbeknownst to the would-be killer) is already dead.

23. THE CLAMOROUS QUAKER

1. 2R 242–47 (CM, 1658).

2. "Leaven" in this context is a figurative term with biblical connotations meaning "an agency which produces profound change by progressive inward operation." 6 OED 166.

3. *Entick v. Carrington*, 19 State Trials 1029 (1765).

4. *Id.*, at 1066.

24. THE CURRIER'S APPRENTICE

1. 1R 250–53 (CM, 1658). A currier is "one whose trade is the dressing and colouring of leather after it is tanned." 2 OED 1271. The trade is distinct from that of the tanner who initially tans the leather.

2. Although modern readers would like to know Wheadon's age, this is a detail we never learn from the text. The records' description of him as an "orphan" and the court's eventual finding that he was legally incapable of making a contract strongly suggest he was young. Exactly how young remains a mystery.

3. 5 OED 199. An apprentice's indenture was, in fact, merely a specific example of a broader set of legal documents, usually deeds, created by lawyers in the days of handwritten documents. "Indentures" were executed in multiple copies with their tops "indented" by a series of cuts, unique to those documents, that would serve to authenticate the documents on future occasions. *See id.*, at 198.

4. It is unclear whether the person who had curried three hides in a day was Wheadon or Meigs.

5. Possibly a variation of "flapdoodle," meaning "nonsense."

6. *See* note 1.

25. THE MILFORD PATERNITY CASE

1. 2R 263–68 (CM, 1658–59).

2. It is unclear whether Sergeant Richard Baldwin was related to the suspect, John Baldwin.

3. Marshall supposedly remarked, "He was a fool of a man that could not have the use of a maid and she not be with child."

4. The reference is to Proverbs 7:6–10. "For at the window of my house I looked through my casement, and beheld among the simple ones, I discerned among the youths, a young man void of understanding, passing through the street near her corner; and he went the way to her house, in the twilight, in the evening, in the black and dark night: And, behold, there met him a woman with the attire of a harlot, and subtil of heart."

5. The first names of these witnesses are not given.

6. These are questions that needed to be asked in the pre-DNA era. In modern times, a DNA test would be ordered, and its results would almost certainly be conclusive on the issue of paternity.

26. THE BRICKMAKER'S APPRENTICE

1. 2R 318–19, 347 (CM, 1659–60). Samuel's surname is spelled "Plum" in the 1659 records and "Plumb" in the 1660 records. The later spelling is used here.

2. John's surname is spelled "Strang" in the 1659 records and "Strange" in the 1660 records. The later spelling is used here.

3. Since we later learn that House's parents were in England, the reference is presumably to a ship transporting House from England to the New World.

4. Since the second indenture was signed on May 1, 1653, House must have been eighteen or nineteen years old at the time of the 1659 hearing.

5. Bloodletting—technically called "venesection"—was thought, from ancient times to the nineteenth century, to be curative of a variety of maladies. According to legend, a treacherous nun bled Robin Hood to death.

6. Brewis is bread soaked in fat dripping from meat. 1 OED 1091. It is still occasionally found on menus in Newfoundland.

27. THE HORSE-TRADING CASE

1. 2R 380–83 (CM, 1660).

2. The records spell the name variably as either "Archer" or "Archers." "Archer" is used here.

3. The exact meaning of this phrase is unclear. Browne later testified that he was unable to find his other horses. The explanation seems to be that the horses were running free and not easily summoned. Browne was waiting for them to "come up" at his command.

4. Some repetitive testimony is omitted.

5. John Baker, VI The Oxford History of the Laws of England 827 (2003).

6. 2 Restatement (Second) of Contracts § 261 (1981).

7. Blount-Midyette & Co. v. Aeroglide Corp., 119 S.E.2d 225 (N.C. 1961).

28. THE MILFORD ARSON CASE

1. 2R 384–87 (CM, 1660–61).

2. The implication of this answer is that Loper usually shared his master's bed. When the master had an overnight guest, the guest got the bed, and Loper, who had no bed of his own, slept on the floor by the fire.

3. It is unclear whether the debt was related to the fires Loper had set.

29. THE SOUTHOLD SLANDER

1. 2R 412–15 (CM, 1661).

2. The meaning of this second charge is unclear.

3. The reference is to Jude 1:8. ("Likewise also these filthy dreamers defile the flesh, despise dominion, and speak evil of dignities.")

30. THE BIGAMIST'S WIFE

1. 2R 425–27 (CM, 1661).

2. Lawrence Stone, *Road to Divorce*, 305–8 (1990).

3. Bigamy was considered a felony but within the "benefit of clergy" (an exemption from capital punishment originally intended for the clergy but later extended to the laity), so the bigamous spouse was likely to be branded rather than hanged. 4 Blackstone 164. Under a 1603 statute (1 Jac. I, c. 11), it was not criminal to remarry if one's spouse had been continually "beyond the Seas" for seven years, but it does not appear that William Andrews waited the prescribed period before marrying his second spouse.

4. 4 Blackstone 163.

31. THE STAMFORD MURDER MYSTERY

1. 2R 458–63, 465, 478 (CM, 1662).

2. The word in the records is "netop." This is the evident meaning of the word.

3. We learn later that the charges are a reference to the costs of keeping Taphanse and the court traveling to Stamford to hear the case.

4. 4 Blackstone 355.

32. THE LECHEROUS SWINEHERD

1. 2R 466–67; MS 328–32 (CM, 1662).

2. Payne and Frost were swineherds. Although modern readers tend to think of pigs as large, indolent animals wallowing in pens, New Haven pigs of the seventeenth century were much friskier animals, which—as the present case repeatedly illustrates—were herded but were always getting lost. Swineherding has been a low-status occupation since biblical times. The Prodigal Son was reduced to tending the pigs prior to his celebrated homecoming (Luke 15:15).

33. THE BURNING BARN

1. 2R 504–10 (CM, 1663).

2. This may have been the ancient judicial practice of "sequestration," still routinely used today. As John Henry Wigmore notes, "The expedient of *separating a party's witnesses*, in order to detect falsehood by exposing inconsistencies, seems to have been early discovered and log practiced in various communities." John Henry Wigmore, 6 Evidence in Trials at Common Law § 1837, at 455 (Chadbourn rev., 1976). The classic story is that of Susanna, told in the Apocrypha, describing the young Daniel's separation (and subsequent demolition) of the one who spoke against Susanna. Goodwife Betts was a witness, and the biblically minded court may have had this precedent in mind. But the court did not routinely sequester witnesses. Plenty of the cases recounted here have featured the appearance of nonsequestered witnesses. Indeed, in this very case, Mary and Hannah Betts are examined in each other's presence. It seems more likely that the court had the less noble goal of depriving two youthful defendants of whatever emotional support their mother might otherwise have provided them.

3. Mary had evidently been held in custody by the marshal.

4. Goodwife Betts has apparently returned to the courtroom.

5. Jasper Crane was a Branford magistrate and a member of the court.

6. The colonies of Massachusetts, New Plymouth, Connecticut, and New Haven had signed Articles of Confederation in 1643. 1R 98.

INDEX

*Unless otherwise specified, towns and colonies referenced
are located in what is now the state of Connecticut.*

Garnet Books

Dennis Barone, editor
*Garnet Poems: An Anthology of
Connecticut Poetry Since 1776**

Michael E. Bell
*Food for the Dead: On the Trail of
New England's Vampires*

Jon C. Blue
*The Case of the Piglet's Paternity:
Trials from the New Haven Colony,
1639–1663**

Peter Bohan and Philip
Hammerslough, Introduction and
Notes by Erin Eisenbarth
Early Connecticut Silver, 1700–1840

Al Braden
*The Connecticut River:
A Photographic Journey through
the Heart of New England*

Susan Campbell
*Tempest-Tossed: The Spirit
of Isabella Beecher Hooker*

James Clark
*Connecticut's Fife &
Drum Tradition**

Brad Davis, editor
Sunken Garden Poetry, 1992–2011

Dan W. DeLuca, editor
*The Old Leather Man:
Historical Accounts of a Connecticut
and New York Legend*

Richard DeLuca
*Post Roads & Iron Horses:
Transportation in Connecticut from
Colonial Times to the Age of Steam**

Anne Farrow
*The Log Books: Connecticut's Slave
Trade and Human Memory**

Dr. Mel Goldstein
Dr. Mel's Connecticut Climate Book

David K. Leff
*Hidden in Plain Sight: A Deep
Traveler Explores Connecticut*

David K. Leff
Maple Sugaring: Keeping It Real in New England

Eric D. Lehman
Becoming Tom Thumb: Charles Stratton, P.T. Barnum, and the Dawn of American Celebrity*

Eric D. Lehman
Homegrown Terror: Benedict Arnold and the Burning of New London*

Laurie Lisle
Westover School: Giving Girls a Place of Their Own

Dione Longley and Buck Zaidel
Heroes for All Time: Connecticut's Civil War Soldiers Tell Their Stories*

Kevin Murphy
Crowbar Governor: The Life and Times of Morgan Gardner Bulkeley*

Kevin Murphy
Fly Fishing in Connecticut: A Guide for Beginners

Kevin Murphy
Water for Hartford: The Story of the Hartford Water Works and the Metropolitan District Commission

Elizabeth J. Normen, editor
African American Connecticut Explored

James F. O'Gorman
Henry Austin: In Every Variety of Architectural Style

Brian O'Rourke
Breakfast at O'Rourke's: New Cuisine from a Classic American Diner

Jon E. Purmont
Ella Grasso: Connecticut's Pioneering Governor*

Jerry Roberts
The British Raid on Essex: The Forgotten Battle of the War of 1812*

Chandler B. Saint and George Krimsky
Making Freedom: The Extraordinary Life of Venture Smith

Leslie Starr
Welcome to Wesleyan: Campus Buildings

Markham Starr
Barns of Connecticut

Renée Tribert and James F. O'Gorman
Gervase Wheeler: A British Architect in America, 1847–1860*

Matthew Warshauer
Connecticut in the American Civil War: Slavery, Sacrifice, and Survival*

Matthew Warshauer
Inside Connecticut and the Civil War: One State's Struggles

Donald E. Williams Jr.
Prudence Crandall's Legacy: The Fight for Equality in the 1830s, Dred Scott, *and* Brown v. Board of Education*

Jelle Zeilinga de Boer
Stories in Stone: How Geology Influenced Connecticut History and Culture

Jelle Zeilinga de Boer and John Wareham
New Haven's Sentinels: The Art and Science of East Rock and West Rock*

FOR MORE INFORMATION ON THE DRIFTLESS CONNECTICUT SERIES, PLEASE VISIT US ONLINE AT HTTP://WWW.WESLEYAN.EDU/WESPRESS/DRIFTLESS

JON C. BLUE
is a judge of the Connecticut Superior Court.
He has written hundreds of judicial opinions and has given
annual lectures on the United States Supreme Court to the
Connecticut Judicial Institute since 1999. Prior to his judicial
appointment, he practiced tax, civil rights, and criminal law.
He lives in Hamden, Connecticut.

About the Driftless Connecticut Series

❦

The Driftless Connecticut Series is a publication award
program established in 2010 to recognize excellent books with
a Connecticut focus or written by a Connecticut author. To be
eligible, the book must have a Connecticut topic or setting or
an author must have been born in Connecticut or have been a
legal resident of Connecticut for at least three years.

The Driftless Connecticut Series is funded by the
Beatrice Fox Auerbach Foundation Fund
at the Hartford Foundation for Public Giving.
For more information and a complete list
of books in the Driftless Connecticut Series,
please visit us online at
http://www.wesleyan.edu/wespress/driftless.